Twayne's English Authors Series

Sylvia E. Bowman, *Editor*

INDIANA UNIVERSITY

Samuel Butler

 2

Samuel Butler

By LEE E. HOLT

American International College

Twayne Publishers, Inc. :: New York

To the memory of HAROLD CLARKE GODDARD,
in whose 1933 seminar
in Modern Literature
at Swarthmore College
I first met Samuel Butler

Preface

This book is not a biography of Samuel Butler—there are abundant biographical studies of Butler, ranging from the two-volume work by Henry Festing Jones through Malcolm Muggeridge's etched-in-acid study to the competent biography by Philip Henderson. Rather, this is a critical summary of Butler's work and an attempt to reevaluate its worth. It is directed to the reader who wishes to know what Butler thought, not how he lived. Since several of Butler's best works are not now generally available, fairly extensive use of quoted passages has seemed advisable to give the true flavor of his writing. Also more space is devoted to summarizing what he wrote than would have been necessary if all his works were better known.

It is impossible, though, to understand Butler's original and stimulating ideas without paying some attention to the man who thought them. I have based my study on certain psychological inferences regarding the genesis of his originality. These seem to me to be almost forced upon anyone who dwells for any length of time on his variegated creative activity, even though some of them, since they have not been consistently worked out before, may appear rather novel in Butler criticism. I hope, however, that my book does not stand or fall with them. I am unaware of having had any specific ax to grind, although obviously I have been influenced by a background of reading in Freud and Jung—quite appropriate reading for studying one of the first of the European authors who made extensive use of the concept of the unconscious.

It seems inevitable when working with Butler to try to understand why he challenged his age in the way he did, why he was both so quarrelsome and in a deeper sense so conciliatory, why he assailed smugness and blind professionalism yet admired almost to idolatry men who are competent and at home in the world. A critical study which ignored these inevitable questions could hardly be considered a critical study at all.

Another type of approach to Butler than mine would have laid greater stress on formal matters—his brilliant use of forensic techniques, his masterly expressiveness, together with his technical innovations in narration. Much has been made recently of the virtuoso use of point of view and "the unreliable narrator" in *The Way of All Flesh.* While I have considered these matters, they have not been my primary concern, and probably much remains to be done in this direction which I have not attempted. My aim has been both more traditional and less abstract: to arouse interest in Butler in terms of his complex of ideas, emotions, hopes, and fears—in short, to expose the content of his time and ours which to me gives his literary odyssey its meaning.

For thirty years now I have worked with Butler off and on, and I do not tire of him. His humor, kindliness, brilliance of mind, and sheer vitality reach through the printed word each time I approach him; my aim in the present study has been to help others to the same experience. It is true that I have not examined all the extensive Butler material available in England, but I have benefited from both Arnold Silver's and Daniel F. Howard's recent publications of Butler's personal correspondence which, they say, is the cream of this material; and I have used the very complete Butler collection in the Chapin Library, Williamstown, Massachusetts, including the original manuscript volumes of the *Note-Books.* I am grateful to the late Carroll A. Wilson and Miss Lucy E. Osborne for letting me use these materials.

I wish to express my grateful thanks also to Mrs. E. Mark Worthen who read my manuscript in its entirety and made many useful suggestions for its improvement; to my wife and to Mrs. Margaret Wittenborg who helped me with their comments on each chapter as I wrote it; and finally thanks must also go to the host of Butler scholars and critics who have aided me in understanding and appreciating his work.

LEE E. HOLT

American International College
October 21, 1963

Quotations from Henry Festing Jones, *Samuel Butler, Author of Erewhon (1835-1902)—a Memoir,* London, 1919, are made with the permission of Macmillan and Co. Ltd.

Contents

Chronology

1835   Samuel Butler born December 4, at Langar Rectory, near Bingham, Nottinghamshire, son of the Reverend Thomas Butler and grandson of Dr. Samuel Butler who was headmaster of Shrewsbury School and Bishop of Lichfield.

1843-   Trip to Italy in the family carriage. Winter in Rome and
1844   Naples. Studied Italian.

1846-   School at Allesley, near Coventry.
1848

1848-   School at Shrewsbury under Dr. Kennedy.
1854

1853-   Second trip to Italy. Continued study of Italian.
1854

1854-   St. John's College, Cambridge. Wrote for *The Eagle.*
1858   Bracketed twelfth in the Classical Tripos.

1857   Vacation trip on the Continent.

1858-   Worked among the poor in London as an amateur lay as-
1859   sistant. Took art lessons.

1859   Gave up idea of ordination. In September, sailed for New Zealand.

1860-   Acquired and managed sheep ranch with £4,200 from his
1864   father. Wrote for *The Press* in Christchurch. Sold ranch; returned to London, having nearly doubled his capital. Began friendship with Charles Paine Pauli.

1863   *A First Year in Canterbury Settlement* published by his father.

1864   Settled at 15 Clifford's Inn, London. Began serious art study at Cary's Art School and at the South Kensington Art School. Painted "Family Prayers."

1865   Published pamphlet on the evidence for the Resurrection. Articles in *The Reasoner.* Trip abroad.

1867 Began attending Heatherley's Art School.

1869- Trip abroad. Met Miss E. M. A. Savage at Heatherley's.
1870 The portrait "Miss Anderson" exhibited at the Royal Academy.

1870- Writing *Erewhon* in his spare time. Articles in *The Drawing Room Gazette*. "A Reverie" exhibited at the Royal Academy.
1871

1872 *Erewhon* published anonymously. Second edition revealed authorship. Writing *The Fair Haven*. Visited Charles Darwin at Down.

1873 *The Fair Haven* published. Death of his mother. Began *The Way of All Flesh*. Invested his capital in Henry Hoare's companies.

1874 "A Child's Head" and "Mr. Heatherley's Holiday" exhibited at the Royal Academy. Henry Hoare's companies failed. Trip to Montreal to salvage his investment. Wrote first passage of *Life and Habit*. Began keeping a systematic notebook.

1875 In Montreal "fighting fraud." Wrote "A Psalm of Montreal." Returned to London in December with £2,000 of his capital left.

1876 "Don Quixote" and "A Girl's Head" exhibited at the Royal Academy. Met Henry Festing Jones. Vacation trip abroad (continued annually through the rest of his life). Work on *Life and Habit*.

1877 Financial worries. Pictures rejected by the Royal Academy. Began using British Museum Reading Room. Gave up attempt to become a professional painter. *Life and Habit* published. Correspondence with Francis Darwin.

1878 Letter to *The Athenaeum* about Ewald Hering's theory concerning biological memory. Canon Butler informed his son that he did not read his books. Work on *The Way of All Flesh* continued. Working on *Evolution, Old and New*.

1879 Articles entitled "A Clergyman's Doubts" and "God the Known and God the Unknown" in the *Examiner*. *Evolution, Old and New* published. Financial crisis. His father rejected his appeal to allow him to borrow on his interest in the Whitehall estate and mansion house left by his grandfather to come to him on his father's and aunt's deaths; £300 annual allowance granted instead. Misunderstanding with Darwin about Ernest Krause's *Kosmos* article, for a translation of which Darwin had provided an introduction.

1880   Letter in *The Athenaeum* calling on Darwin for an explanation; none given until 1911, after Butler's death. Was offered £100 for a book on Italy. *Unconscious Memory* published.

1881   Threatened legal proceedings forced *Nature* to print his letter presenting case against Darwin. Given absolute revision to Whitehall property; financial distress eased. *Alps and Sanctuaries of Piedmont and the Canton Ticino* published.

1882   New edition of *Evolution, Old and New*. Death of Darwin. Lectured on memory at the Working Men's College.

1883   Wrote first music. Working on *The Way of All Flesh*.

1884   *Selections from Previous Works* published. Correspondence in *The Athenaeum* about Romanes and *Life and Habit*. Work on *Narcissus: a Cantata in the Handelian Form* with Jones. Spoke at the Linnean Society.

1885   Death of Miss Savage. Work on *Luck, or Cunning?* *Gavottes, Minuets and Fugues* published.

1886   Bellini and Holbein articles in *The Athenaeum*. Unsuccessful application for the Slade Professorship of Art at Cambridge. *Luck, or Cunning, as the Main Means of Organic Modification?* published. *Narcissus: a Cantata in the Handelian Form* performed. Death of his father.

1887   Alfred Emery Cathie engaged as clerk. Jones given a stipend. Lectured at the Working Men's College. Banquet in Butler's honor at Varallo.

1888   *Ex Voto* published. *Narcissus: a Cantata in the Handelian Form* published. Began a series of eight articles for the *Universal Review*.

1889   Working on life of his grandfather.

1890   Studying counterpoint with Rockstro. Lecture at the Working Men's College on "Thought and Language." Working on *Ulysses*, an oratorio, with Jones.

1891   Translating the *Odyssey*. Continued work on life of his grandfather and an Italian edition of *Ex Voto*. Revising notebooks.

1892   First visit to Sicily. Lecture at the Working Men's College on "The Humour of Homer." Letters in *The Athenaeum* on typography of the *Odyssey*.

1893   "L'Origine Siciliana dell' Odissea" and "On the Trapanese Origin of the *Odyssey*" published. Explorations in Italy and Sicily. Friendship with a Swiss student, Hans Faesch, who was visiting London.

1894   *Ex Voto* published in Italian. *Life of Dr. Butler* rejected by Cambridge Press and by Oxford Press. *Odyssey* translation rejected by thirty publishers. Translating the *Iliad*.

1895   Visit to Greece and the Troad. The Swiss student Hans Faesch left London. Wrote "In Memoriam H. R. F." Suffering from poor health and tension. Shortening the rejected *Life of Dr. Butler*. Letters to *The Academy* about the art of writing in the time of Homer.

1896   *The Life and Letters of Dr. Samuel Butler* published at Butler's risk. Unsuccessful attempts to get Homer translations published at publisher's risk.

1897   *The Authoress of the Odyssey* refused by Murray and G. Bell and Sons under any conditions; published by Longman's at Butler's risk. Death of Pauli.

1898   *The Iliad Rendered into English Prose* published. Learned Shakespeare's sonnets by heart. Letter to *The Athenaeum* about the dating of the sonnets.

1899   *Shakespeare's Sonnets Reconsidered and in Part Rearranged* published.

1900   *The Odyssey Rendered into English Prose* published. Work on *Erewhon Revisited*.

1901   *Erewhon Revisited* rejected by Longmans; published by Grant Richards with help from George Bernard Shaw. Revised edition of *Erewhon*. Failing health. Arranging correspondence, especially Miss Savage's letters.

1902   Sonnet "Not on Sad Stygian Shore" in *The Athenaeum*. Arranging correspondence. Letter to the *Spectator* about 1872 review of *Erewhon*. New edition of *Ex Voto* rejected by Longmans and by Grant Richards. Proposed new book on Tabachetti. Death on June 18.

1903   *The Way of All Flesh* published.

1912   *The Note-Books of Samuel Butler* published.

1923-1926   *The Shrewsbury Edition* published in twenty volumes.

"Perhaps a little bit of absolute truth on any one question might prove a general solvent, and dissipate the universe."

"Logic is like the sword. Those that appeal to it shall perish by it."

SAMUEL BUTLER in The Note-Books

"The so-called man of science . . . is but medicine-man, augur, priest, in its latest development; useful it may be, but requiring to be well watched by those who value freedom."

SAMUEL BUTLER in Life and Habit

Samuel Butler

CHAPTER 1

First Steps

I *Preliminary Considerations*

AMONG the sterling qualities of the work of Samuel Butler are its ability to raise questions; its capacity to give pleasure with its lucid, humorous, vivid prose; and its power to challenge us to greater honesty with ourselves. It demands so much candor and openness of the reader that not everyone can rise to meet it —certainly, most of Butler's contemporaries could not. This man, who once herded sheep in New Zealand and who was also a painter, composer of music, satirist, novelist, art critic, science writer, classicist, poet, and journalist, lived away from publicity and fame and devoted himself to preparing a literary feast.

Why did he do so? [1] Surely not merely, as he humorously suggested, that he might have something to read in his old age! Moreover, his background does not explain his achievements. Many a man has refused, like Butler, to follow the path his father marked out for him, but for most of them nothing has come of this rebellion. Butler, however, rejected not only his father but the stereotypes of his own age as well; and, unlike other rebels, he created a world of ideas which lives today more vividly than when he created it. We shall attempt to discover what led him to strike out on his very original career. [2]

Butler achieved what he achieved with little encouragement save from the poor, lame ex-governess Miss Eliza Mary Ann Savage, who alone recognized his ability and gloried in it. Why, we must surely ask, did he devote so much of his career to writing seventeen volumes, all but three of which he published at his own expense, [3] and all but two of which failed to win much of an audience in his lifetime? Not only this, but he even prepared additional material which was published after his death. Surely the force and originality of these volumes prove that he was right to insist so stubbornly on charting his own way. The courage that led him to write cannot have come merely from the conviction that everyone can be creative if he will persevere in working at the task nearest to hand. Perhaps his goal was to realize a set of convictions which would free him from the inhibitions hampering other men.

Of course Butler made renunciations to achieve what he wanted to achieve—such is the requirement of life. But the significant fact is that he found sufficient security to dispense with the fear of "giving himself away." His "incarnate bachelorhood," [4] his carefully organized life, the areas of thought and feeling to which he could not trust himself—all these were bulwarks against the inner originality which he had to control and to channel in order to save himself. A passage in *Life and Habit,* which Butler tells us embodies the original idea for that book and which came to him as he listened to the bells in Montreal,[5] gives a clue to the problem of achieving the unity in diversity for which he strove, and which he saw as the ideal for all men:

His past selves are living in unruly hordes within him at this moment and overmastering him. "Do this, this, this, which we too have done, and found our profit in it," cry the souls of his forefathers within him. Faint are the far ones, coming and going as the sound of bells wafted on to a high mountain; loud and clear are the near ones, urgent as an alarm of fire. "Withhold," cry some. "Go on boldly," cry others. "Me, me, me, revert hitherward, my descendant," shouts one as it were from some high vantage-ground over the heads of the clamorous multitude. "Nay, but me, me, me," echoes another; and our former selves fight within us and wrangle for our possession. (43)[6]

Some critics have accused Butler of lacking the tragic sense of life;[7] rather, it might be said that tragedy not in its well understood classical sense but in some new, not yet comprehended shape, was so near him that he had to be systematic, even petty on occasion, to keep it at bay. Excessively orderly people sometimes shield a chaos within. Butler's neat conformity in later years to the gentlemanly life protected his right to risk his all on his unrecognized, unacclaimed odyssey of creation. His possessiveness, his need to relate everything to his own ego which P. N. Furbank has so effectively pointed out,[8] may have sprung—as it seems to have done with Beethoven[9] and many others—from the necessity of preserving himself from the incursions of originality. It might also be the result of his firm refusal to accede to conventional standards of judgment, of his conviction that our primary responsibility is to know what our real selves want. He was brewing a heady mixture in his vats. Thus he had to exercise a meticulous control made up of fastidious notebook entries and of careful relations with people, things, money, and emotions; he had to keep the unknown from overwhelming him; instead, he had to turn it into a kind of curative art for mankind. That through him so much of the unknown did turn into curative art is a measure of his success.

II *The Beginning*

The reader of Samuel Butler's writing will do well to remember that he had a distinct English pride of family and position. It was not that he wanted to tolerate snobbishness or to give in thoughtlessly to tradition. He simply became convinced, even as he suffered from his own rebellion which led to some of his keenest insights, that for the happiness and peace that will allow a man to devote his energies to important work it is necessary to have inherited tradition (the bells) quietly cooperating rather than in revolt against one. The outraged voices on the boardinghouse stairs in the nightmare Raskolnikov has after the commission of his crime in Dostoevsky's *Crime and Punishment*[10] dramatize the anguish of inherited but violated ideals. The voices represent in literary symbolism the kind of disruption which Butler came to discover he must avoid, especially because he saw that his thoughts forced upon him a crime against tradition. So he revered the man who had these traditions and ideals healthily in hand, and he did more to keep them in hand in his own life than is admitted by critics who have wished to exploit the revolutionary in him.

Henry Festing Jones traces the Butler family tree back to 1580 and reveals a whole pattern of surrounding figures to whom Butler could relate his revolt and of whom he remained always highly conscious.[11] "Stone House" in Kenilworth, which stayed in the family until 1891, had been lived in by descendants of an eighteenth-century Samuel Butler who was the steward to Lord Clarendon and Lord Leigh; there was a James Butler, surgeon, engineer, artist, who traveled widely and died in the East Indies; then there was Dr. Samuel Butler, headmaster of Shrewsbury,

Bishop of Lichfield, and grandfather of our Butler. Between 1889 and 1896 Butler wrote a biography of this famous schoolmaster in two large volumes, and he became genuinely intrigued by the scholar-teacher who, on close acquaintance, he found far from being the horror his imagination had formerly painted.[12] Butler's life was lived in constant relation, sometimes good, often bad, with his father, his mother, his two sisters, his brother Thomas, and a host of other relatives close and distant. He did indeed make fun of these relatives in conversation with his cronies, Miss Savage and Henry Festing Jones, and in his writing; but he also was most kind to them in his letters, his careful observance of punctilio, his calls upon them. He did not publish *The Way of All Flesh* during his lifetime because he desired to spare their feelings.[13]

The seeds of revolt sprouted in Butler in spite of himself. In part they grew as a protest against cruelty and against the tyranny of parents over children, of profession over vocation, of the straitjacket of formal life. Mrs. R. S. Garnett and others have viewed Butler's rebellion as unwarranted;[14] one critic describes Victorian family life as the happiest on record.[15] Both miss the point. Butler was not so much excoriating his own family life, or the life of an age—however much he drew on both for the details of his picture—as he was defending the principle of freedom. He was crying out in outrage over the maiming wounds inflicted by all insensitivity, all tyranny, all intellectual dogmatism. That he cried out because he had felt these things himself or because they were particularly Victorian is beside the point. Linked with Theobald's callous beating of the infant Ernest for pronouncing *come* as *tum* (*The Way of All Flesh*, 96) is the injustice of the attempt to force Ernest into the clergy when he feels no call to live a life of what, for him, would be hypocrisy and sham. The two are equally bad, and both might happen in any age.

The rebellion in Butler seems to have started early and to have grown apace, and no doubt the details in his novel tell us much about it. Yet Butler seems to have progressed well enough as a student at Shrewsbury and at Cambridge though, like Thoreau, he later accused the universities of teaching nothing of importance. In *Alps and Sanctuaries,* Butler says: "I was very happy at Cambridge. . . . I shall ever retain a most kindly recollection both of Cambridge and of the school where I passed my boyhood; but I feel . . . that I have spent as much of my maturer years in unlearning as in learning" (134). Yet, again like Thoreau, he made excellent use of what he learned, particularly of the classics, the "hypothetical language" of Erewhon. His father had thrashed Latin grammar into him, beginning when he was four, until he knew all the rules by heart,[16] and he graduated from Cambridge twelfth in the Classical Tripos in 1858.[17] Also at Cambridge he wrote for the first time for publication: *The Eagle,* a magazine "written and edited by members of St. John's College, Cambridge" (*A First Year* . . . , 3), printed his two essays, "On English Composition and Other Matters" and "Our Tour."

In the piece on composition he states a conviction that stuck with him and influenced his own writing: "the style of our authors of a couple of hundred years ago was more terse and masculine than that of those of the present day, possessing both more of the graphic element, and more vigour, straightforwardness, and conciseness." He then adds: "a man should be clear of his meaning before he endeavours to give it any kind of utterance, and . . . having made up his mind what to say, the less thought he takes how to say it, more than briefly, pointedly, and plainly, the better" (3). Here is his first move toward independence; at the start of his career he rejects the style of his age. And he was right to do so. Butler in his best passages achieves a clarity and succinctness most unvictorian. Also, he refuses to find the process of expression mysterious, though it should be noted that to write "briefly, pointedly, and plainly" is not so easy as he implies. Butler's own painstaking and continual revisions of the materials for his notebooks testify to this difficulty. Nevertheless, he remained a lifelong enemy of "fine writing."

Butler had visited Italy, the country which was to mean so much to him, with his family in 1843 and 1853; in 1857 he went there again with a college friend, and his account of this brief trip was his second publication in *The Eagle.* "Our Tour" reflects the high spirits of a youthful excursion. A passage in it involving a memory from his earlier tour is especially meaningful for one who was to expend so much effort crossing boundaries. The passage describes a crossing through a tunnel from one side of a mountain range to the other: "All was the same [as on his present trip]—bitter cold, dense fog, and ever silently increasing hoarfrost: but on emerging from it [the tunnel], the whole scene was completely changed; the air was clear, the sun shining brightly, no hoar-frost and only a few patches of fast melting snow . . ." (11). As we read this we think of the hero of *Erewhon* crossing the range into his unknown kingdom. Even more, we think of the concluding passage of Chapter 28, "The Escape": ". . . the light of the afternoon sun welcomes him as he leaves the tunnel, and behold a smiling valley—a babbling brook, a village with tall belfries, and meadows of brilliant green—these are the things which greet him, and he smiles to himself as the terror passes away. . . ." [18]

Canon Joseph McCormick, who knew Butler well at Cambridge, kept some short sketches Butler wrote while an undergraduate; these eleven pieces—published in *A First Year in Canterbury Settlement*—again reveal the good spirits and humor of their author. One is a satire on translations, supposedly from Herodotus: "In this way then the Johnians, I say, practise their tub" (28); another presents scenes from Cambridge life for the shield of Achilles; a third describes the methods to be used to create friction and disunion among friends, ways "of producing, fostering, and invigorating strife of all kinds, whereby the society of man will be profited much" (31). Some will remark that Butler spent his life trying to carry out this youthful proposal! Then there is the ironic advice of a father to his son about how to achieve power in the world—put love of self above all else. There is also the typical takeoff on Latin in a skit describing Thomas Bridges' application for the position of shoeblack, followed by the qualifying examinations the authorities set him: "Prove that the shoe may be represented by an equation of the fifth degree. Find the equation to a man blacking a shoe: (1) in rectangular co-ordinates; (2) in polar co-ordinates," etc. (43). In addition there is a humorous description in verse of two deans and a brief drama in which the deans, after complimenting Butler for his piety, are shocked to see him cross the courtyard without gown or cap, bearing a cup, a bottle of cider, lemons, nutmegs, and sugar (49).

III *Revolt and Escape*

It is hard today to believe that so recently as 1854-1858 Butler, a Cambridge student, had "never met any one who entertained a doubt" of the Christian miracles.[19] Yet Butler himself suggests that this was so (*Collected Essays*, I, 55).[20] Since he was intending to enter the ministry, however, he was thinking about religion, as is evidenced by a broadside he wrote spoofing the evangelical Simeonites. This broadside may have been placed in the Simeonites' mailboxes, as was the one written by Ernest Pontifex. It is scornful of those who take religion too seriously, and it reflects the conflict in the Church of England between the High Church and the Evangelical parties. It also suggests Butler's lifelong suspicion of zealotry. "Men are disgusted with religion," it concludes, "if it is placed before them at unseasonable times, in unseasonable places, and clothed in a most unseemly dress. . . . A whited sepulchre . . . is an acknowledged humbug, and most of the Sims are not, in my opinion, very far different" (*A First Year . . . ,* 59).

Jones tells us that, in preparing for ordination, Butler attempted to ascertain his own reasons for being a Christian.[21] He made a close study of the New Testament in Greek and of the commentators on it; he also worked in London after his graduation as an amateur lay assistant among the poor. When he found, however, that there was no distinction in conduct and character between the boys in his evening class who had been baptized and those who had not,[22] his faith in dogma was destroyed,[23] and he decided not to be ordained. The emphasis given this experience in various of Butler's books suggests that it was no doubt in part a rationalization of a deeper revolt. But it carried much conviction in the nineteenth century.

When Butler announced his decision to his family, all of them were filled with consternation. The choice of professions for the son of a class-conscious father in 1859 was narrower than it would be today. His father immediately wrote to him threatening to cut off all financial support unless he reconsidered his rejection of the ministry, entered the bar, or became a schoolmaster.[24] Butler, however, had already set his heart on becoming an artist. He had begun to take art lessons and was working diligently. Nevertheless, he offered to compromise by studying medicine, by emigrating, or by becoming a farmer in England. His father said *no* to these suggestions. Samuel then announced his intention of getting along without further parental support. "I have duties to myself to perform," he wrote, "even more binding on me than those to my parents." [25] But he begged for continuing friendship with his family: "I should be very sorry to think that any other connection

than the money connection should cease," he wrote, and "I trust
. . . that I shall be allowed to correspond with Langar [his family's home]." [26] He refused to make his life "a lie and a sham" [27] by
entering a profession he did not believe in simply to please his
parents and to win their support.

The matter was finally settled by compromise on the Reverend
Thomas Butler's part: young Samuel was sent to New Zealand in
September of 1859, his passage was paid, and he was promised a
sum of £5,200 to get himself established, of which eventually,
after some further misunderstandings, £4,200 was paid.[28] On the
night of his departure, Butler for the first time in his life did not
say his prayers. He never said them again.[29] During the voyage he
read Gibbon, a writer notorious in Victorian days for his cynical
account of the early development of Christianity.[30]

The years 1860-1864, spent in New Zealand, were crucial in
tempering Butler's nature. On his own in a new environment, he
could rub shoulders with all kinds of people; and he could find
out how to manage a considerable sum of money and a special
kind of industry—sheep raising—so as to come out ahead. When
he left New Zealand he had increased his capital to £8,200.[31]

Butler's first book was published as the direct result of his father's pride in his emigrant son. G. D. H. Cole observes that
Canon Butler's being "at the pains of making a book out of his
son's letters home from New Zealand, of seeking out a publisher
for them, and thus of giving his son his first impetus towards a
literary career" shows that he was not "so set against his son, or
so determined to thwart him, as Butler was accustomed to make
out." [32] His father combined Butler's letters home with material
from two articles Butler had sent to Cambridge for publication in
The Eagle,[33] wrote a brief preface, and had the whole printed
under the title of *A First Year in Canterbury Settlement* (1863).
Although it appears that Butler himself never liked this book,[34]
probably because it accepts the world of reality naïvely at its face
value, it makes very lively reading. Written in a clear, narrative
style and full of detailed accounts of the problems faced by the
settlers in New Zealand, *A First Year* . . . has a freshness and a
nonintrospective happiness that smack of the new world.

When reading Butler's later books, it is well to remember first
that he got his start in a frontier society where each person was
expected to stand up for what he believed, and second that Can-

terbury Settlement itself had been projected in 1850 as a kind of Christian Utopia. Butler notes with admiration the healthy appearance of the pioneers, their odd turns of phrase, the way they identify themselves with their sheep, and their basic shrewdness. He is attacked by the yen of the explorer: "As soon as I saw the mountains, I longed to get on the other side of them" (98), and he is proud of himself for roughing it so well. He describes the men living on the frontier as having a life that "appears a kind of mixture of that of a dog and that of an emperor, with a considerable predominance of the latter" (99). "There is much nonsense in the old country," he says, "from which people here are free. There is little conventionalism, little formality, and much liberality of sentiment; very little sectarianism . . ." (101).[35] Especially he enjoys his trips of exploration up several valleys looking for new sheep land. The scenery that unfolds before him is precisely the scenery he later describes in the account of Higgs's trip over the range in *Erewhon* (xv).

But Butler's life during his four years in New Zealand was not so primitive or free as the account in *The First Year . . .* suggests. Joseph Jones in *The Cradle of Erewhon*[36] tells us that once Butler had established his sheep run at Mesopotamia, New Zealand, he spent much time at Christchurch. He joined the Christchurch Club and came to know practically everyone of importance in the town. He rode with the top political dignitaries on the first trip of the railroad between Christchurch and Lyttleton. Considering the primitive conditions of his ranch, it is surprising that he took a piano there, dragging it on his dray with bullocks. Robert B. Booth in his *Five Years in New Zealand* says about a period he spent working for Butler: "Butler, Cook, and I would repair to the sitting-room [after supper] and round a glorious fire smoked or read or listened to Butler's piano. It was the most civilized experience I had had of up-country life." [37] L. J. Kennaway in *Crusts* describes Butler as "an explorer, who had seen some very hard times, and who, inside a sunburnt and wrinkled forehead, possessed far-thinking and acute brains." [38]

Butler himself was aware of the effect of his new experience. "A wider circle of ideas has resulted from travel," he writes to a friend, "and an entire uprooting of all past habits has been accompanied with a hardly less entire change of opinions upon many subjects. Firstly, I have lost all desire of making other people think the same as myself." [39] Again, he states: "I think I am a Unitarian now, but don't know and won't say; as for the Trinity I cannot make head or tail of it." [40] A year later he says: "For the present I renounce Christianity altogether. . . . I can only say that I have not found my digestion impeded since I have left off believing in what does not appear to be supported by sufficient evidence." [41]

IV *The Kettle Boils*

In 1861 a newspaper called *The Press* was founded in Christchurch by James Edward FitzGerald, an intimate friend of Butler's. Like *The Eagle* at Cambridge, it became an outlet for occasional pieces by Butler who, Jones tells us,[42] was on one occasion in charge of it for some months during the editor's absence.

On December 20, 1852, *The Press* printed a dialogue by Butler entitled "Darwin on the Origin of Species." Purporting to be a discussion between two men who have read Darwin's book, one who liked it and one who did not, it is a clear, succinct statement of Darwin's chief arguments, combined with a cleverly dramatized but only slightly developed opposition to them. "C" (the critic) complains of Darwin's logicality, his monomania, his coldness, and his heartlessness, and concludes that he is "horrid" and "utterly subversive of Christianity." Could it be that "C" stands for "Cellarius," the pen name Butler had used in *The Eagle* and was to use again? "F" (the defender) points out that the struggle for survival is indeed ruthless, but he states that he believes in both Christianity and Darwin. Since they appear to be irreconcilable, "the true course" must be "to use the freest candour in the acknowledgement of the difficulty; to estimate precisely its real value, and obtain a correct knowledge of its precise form. Then and then only is there a chance of any satisfactory result being obtained" (*A First Year* . . . , 194).

Which of the two voices is Butler's? In a way, this is an unanswerable question: Since Butler created them both, he must have understood what each was saying; the issue is not resolved, only dramatized. Nevertheless, the impression was conveyed to many, including Darwin who somehow came into possession of a copy of the article, that it was a defense of, rather than an attack upon, the new theory of evolution. On March 24, 1863, Darwin sent a copy of the article to the editor of a magazine in England with the suggestion that—because it was "remarkable from its spirit and from giving so clear and accurate a view" of his theory —it deserved reprinting.[43]

According to Butler, three responses to his piece in *The Press* were probably written by Charles John Abraham, Bishop of Wellington (186). The first of these considers the Darwinian theory nothing "but a *réchaufée* of the old story that his namesake, Dr. Darwin, served up in the end of the last century" (196); and it objects to the fact that Darwin's "fantasias . . . are made to come around at last to religious questions, with which really and truly they have nothing to do" (197). Butler, who replied in a letter signed "A.M.," criticized his own dialogue as rash, self-satisfied, and uninformed; and he then labeled the argument of his critic "disgraceful," pointing out that there is nothing about natural selection in the elder Darwin's work. Finally, he appealed to the reader to withhold judgment on the new theory until the experts themselves had decided whether it was true or not (198-201).

Butler's concealment of his authorship of the original dialogue when writing again is typical. He liked best to work dramatically with ideas to see how far they would go; already he was intrigued by the methods of thought, by the drama of conflict. It is hard to believe that even in 1863 he would have been willing to defer uncritically to the opinion of experts, but he could certainly envision his argument as something which would tell in a debate. Indeed, a trap lies open for any reader of Butler who concludes from a single statement he may make that this is his considered opinion, even at the time he makes it. Very often Butler is merely testing his reader.

A letter signed "The Savoyard," which followed three weeks later, gives a quotation from the elder Darwin's *Botanic Garden* which implies a theory of natural selection (though teleological, not fortuitous, as Charles' essentially was); and it may very well have been instrumental in drawing Butler's attention to aspects of the earlier evolutionist's work of which he was yet unaware. Four days later Butler replied. Evidently he had not yet recognized the difference between the two natural selections. But, as he was later to show, even Charles Darwin himself did not successfully separate them. Indeed, many thinkers were occupied the rest of the nineteenth century in working out this distinction. Butler pointed out to "The Savoyard" that Dr. Darwin's views were nothing but a speculation, whereas Charles Darwin had gathered evidence for a well-organized theory which could be appraised by the scientific world.

On June 13 Butler again contributed to *The Press*. This piece was entitled "Darwin among the Machines" and was signed "Cellarius." Perhaps in the interim he had been meditating on the mechanical nature of the Darwinian theory which allows only for chance variations; in any case, this is the initial treatment of an idea exploited fully in *Erewhon*, namely that machines themselves can be seen undergoing an evolutionary process from simple to complex. They get more and more efficient as the years pass. And some even have rudimentary organs. The article suggests that these machines may very well be man's successors: ". . . we are daily giving them greater power and supplying by all sorts of ingenious contrivances that self-regulating, self-acting power which will be to them what intellect has been to the human race. In the course of ages we shall find ourselves the inferior race" (210). Thus man, Butler suggests, will continue to exist, but only as the servant of the machine. Eventually, he speculates, machines will develop so far that they will be able to reproduce themselves. Already, he says, one machine is often employed in making another. Since, therefore, it is perfectly evident that if machines are allowed to continue to develop they will dominate the world, he calls for war to the death against them. "Every machine of every sort should be destroyed. . . . Let there be no exceptions made, no quarter shown. . . . If it be urged that this is impossible under the present condition of human affairs, this at once proves that the mischief is already done, that our servitude has commenced in good earnest" (212-13).

Here for the first time is heard the clear voice of the rebel in Butler. Kill the machines! Kill the mindless, loveless universe which, like despotic fathers, threatens to destroy us all! The kettle was beginning to boil. The twenty-eight-year-old Butler had rejected his father's plans for his career. He had partly won his way. Though he was not studying art as he had wished, he was at least on his own in a new country. Now he was beginning the metaphysical speculation about the meaning of life which was to occupy him increasingly as the years went by. He was searching for a new father in the form of a universe in which a man could live, a meaningful, warm one—not one tyrannized by senseless, mechanical creations, by beings derived by chance. A man whose mind could play so brilliantly with ideas, who could stir up troubles where others were content to find none, and who could reevaluate religion, ethics, and evolutionary theory—such a man might well need somewhere along the line to call a truce with probing logic. Did a sense of brooding superiority, an assumption of a complete father role for himself, cause him henceforth to smile a little condescendingly even at his own ideas? Or did he become funny because he was afraid? "Cellarius" concludes his piece with a deprecatory twist: "For the present, we shall leave this subject, which we present gratis to the members of the Philosophical Society. Should they consent to avail themselves of the vast field which we have pointed out, we shall endeavour to labour in it ourselves at some future and indefinite period" (213).

Joseph Jones speculates that a sarcastic review of *A First Year* . . . , published in *The Press* for April 28, 1863, is by Butler too. It seems more plausible, however, to regard this article as the first of the series of critical notices which plagued Butler throughout his life and which also strengthened his determination not to attend to the opinion of the world around him. "The vein of glib self-satisfaction and thinly concealed conceit which runs through the whole volume," the reviewer says, "must render it almost amusingly nauseous even to the most charitable reader." [44]

V *The Return*

By 1864 Butler was beginning to feel able once again to face the threats to his identity from which he had escaped. He seems to have gleaned what happiness he could from the easy, extroverted frontier society that surrounded him and to have grown increasingly dissatisfied with its lack of depth. He became convinced, too, that land values in New Zealand would fall and that, if he waited too long before he sold his sheep run, he might not make out well; subsequent events proved him right. So, on June 15, he left his new life to return to London and the old. For some time, however, he kept at the back of his mind the thought that he might eventually return for reinforcement, but he never did. There is no evidence at this stage of his career that he contemplated literature as a possible profession.

The £8,200 he had amassed from the sale of his New Zealand

holdings Butler invested at ten per cent interest in the colony, for he intended to live on the income. Returning with him to England at his expense was Charles Paine Pauli, a subeditor of *The Press*, whom he had befriended. Butler continued to assist Pauli financially until Pauli's death in 1897, although for many years he could ill afford to do so. He had one of the major shocks of his life when he eventually discovered that Pauli had been sponging on him mercilessly during years when he had actually been in no need whatever of financial assistance.[45] Sensing the possibility within himself for being exploited, which this friendship and the even more disastrous episode of his ill-advised financial speculations in Henry Hoare's companies proved an only too painful reality, Butler developed a stronger and stronger insistence upon the importance of worldly wisdom and shrewdness in money matters. These qualities, he felt, are part of the defense mechanism the man of imagination must erect to give him the freedom he needs in order to create.

On his arrival in London, Butler moved into the quarters at 15 Clifford's Inn which he was to occupy for the rest of his life. He immediately took up a simple routine of living that would allow him to do the work he wanted to do. His ambition at this time, and until 1877, was to prove that he had been right in desiring to become a painter. Attending art school and laboring many hours in the studio in his quarters, he worked diligently and long at this endeavor. The picture "Family Prayers" (*The Way of All Flesh*, Frontispiece), one of the first products of his renewed ambition, shows eight adults expressing varying degrees of boredom as they sit in the living room of his father's home listening to a paterfamilias (a clergyman) read from the Bible. Significant is the fact that none of the portraits seem to be of Butler's family or friends, but this picture is certainly a forestudy for *The Way of All Flesh*. Butler noted that if he had continued to paint out of his head, as he did in this picture, rather than to make academic studies from models, he "would have been all right." [46]

VI *More Darwinian Speculations*

But he did not neglect his writing. Several months after his return to London he sent to the editors of *The Press* (July 29, 1865) another article inspired by Darwinism called "Lucubratio Ebria." So tentative is his approach to the ideas proposed that he makes the suggestion that they may be nothing but a drunken dream. This allows him to spin out an amusing opening paragraph, but it may also reflect his own puzzlement over the intriguing thoughts that his mind had conceived. Again he hides his identity; again he attacks his own previous contribution, "Darwin among the Machines." But this time he defends an opposite point of view: He argues that machines, rather than being threats to the supremacy of mankind, are "the mode of development by which [the] human organism is most especially advancing, and every fresh invention is to be considered as an additional member of the resources of the human body" (*A First Year* . . . , 217). This argument is based on the assumption that "The limbs of the lower animals have never been modified by any act of deliberation and forethought on their own part," but that, "when human intelligence stole like a late spring upon the mimicry of our semi-simious ancestry, the creature learnt how he could of his own forethought add extra-corporaneous limbs to the members of his own body" (215).

In a sense, Butler is probing the implications of a mechanically operated survival-of-the-fittest theory and is reducing it to absurdity. Why cannot machines be organisms, if organisms themselves have evolved by a mindless chance? Henceforth, Butler suggests, we might evaluate people on the relative complexity of their organization. A "really well-developed specimen of the race . . . will be furnished with a large box upon wheels, two horses, and a coachman" (218). In conclusion, though, he admits that there are other modes of judging men beside the organizational one. "Were we to go into this part of the question we should never have done," he says, "and we are compelled reluctantly to leave our dream in its present fragmentary condition" (220).

Butler restated the thesis of his "Darwin among the Machines" in "The Mechanical Creation," which appeared in *The Reasoner* (July 1, 1865) in London. In it, as in "Lucubratio Ebria," he refers to his ideas as "half-shadow, half-substance," and says that he will leave "the intelligent reader to draw his own inferences" (231). He opens by suggesting that the form that future life may take is as difficult for men to imagine as animal life might have been for an observer who saw the world inhabited by nothing but plants. But, crossing the boundary that this suggests, he says that we may be living "in the first faint dawning" (232) of a new life which will be as different from men as they are from the vegetables. He argues that the rapid evolution of machines leading up to the steam engine which eats, breathes, and regulates itself is a clue to what is to come. "It cannot be said to be conscious, but the strides which it has made are made in the direction of consciousness" (233).

This article ends on a calmer note than did "Darwin among the Machines." Instead of calling for a revolt against machines before it is too late to stop their triumphant progress, Butler admits that, since personal advantage rightly dictates to each generation what it does, mankind must resign itself to a future in which it will be well treated by its machine masters who will require the services of men but will of necessity have evolutionary supremacy over them. At the end of the article he promises in a future piece "to regard machinery as a component part of the human organism" (237); he apparently meant to rework "Lucubratio Ebria" for his London audience.

VII *New Departures*

A month later, however, Butler moved in a different direction. In a piece called "Precaution in Free Thought" published by *The Reasoner* (August 1, 1865), Butler grapples with the evolution of opinion (238-41). He takes the conservative position, one which seems to be becoming a necessity for him. He argues that although each generation must find out for itself its standard of right and should do what it can "to advance it in defiance of the world," care must be taken not to push for a growth which the roots will not support: "A sudden change of creed, unless a man is very clear indeed as to the steps by which he has changed it, is not unlikely to do him as much harm as good" (239). Referring specifically to the arguments for Christian miracles—which Jones states had concerned Butler in his university and New Zealand days—[47] he remarks that there must be a "screw loose" in every intellect which believes them.

Butler, nonetheless, points out that—since to deny these arguments is to bring a charge of stupidity, indolence, and cowardice against the age—one must proceed with great caution: "Loss of faith in the general right-mindedness and clear-headedness of one's age is a much more serious thing than loss of faith in a personal Deity" (240). Butler is thus telling himself, as well as his readers, to be cautious in the development of ideas, since solidarity is an essential hedge against insanity. A characteristic comment in this article is his observation that it is more dangerous to be opposed to the wealth of the country than to its thought: "It [wealth] is an august symbol. The universities, the public schools, the rampant Sabbatarianism of the age, the countless churches, the huge organizations of the various Christian creeds, are visible signs of one's own audacity" (239). Butler was becoming aware of what he himself would be in for as his career developed.

That Butler's doubts about religion were as important to him at this time as his exploration of the implications of Darwinism is shown by his printing at his own expense (his first venture into this kind of publication) a pamphlet called "The Evidence for the Resurrection of Jesus Christ as Given by the Four Evangelists, Critically Examined," much of which he incorporated into *The Fair Haven* (1873).[48] In the preface to the pamphlet, he questions the sincerity of an age in which "no publisher of position will publish heresy so rank as mine," [49] even though he is conscious of having done nothing more than to reason logically. Why cannot honest arguments be met by honest replies? He blames no one in particular: "No publisher of position can make them [Butler's arguments] public, even if he would, without doing himself a greater injury than he would be warranted in doing." [50]

As subsequent events were to show, Butler was not to give up the attempt to get a hearing for his ideas. If direct statement went unheeded, he was shortly to try indirect statement, humor, and satire. He was also to seek to deepen his understanding of the reasons mankind could not tolerate a direct approach or a too rigid logic, so that he might learn to eschew these things himself. As Jones points out,[51] this pamphlet was Butler's apology for refusing to become a clergyman. At this point in his life he needed to get his reasons clearly stated. Interesting is the fact that Darwin, who read the pamphlet, wrote Butler: "I particularly agree with all you say in your preface." [52]

CHAPTER 2

Over the Range

I *A New Profession*

IN 1870, at the advice of his doctor, Butler took an extended vacation on the Continent. In Venice he became acquainted with a Russian lady who on his departure said, "Et maintenant, Monsieur, vous allez créer." Butler's comment in his notes is: "Yes, but how to create? and what? I had not yet, for all my education, got to know that doing is the sole parent of doing, and creating a little the only way of learning how to create more; still, I went home resolved to do at any rate something in literature, if not in painting." Another push toward literature came from Sir Frederick Napier Broome, who, visiting England from New Zealand, called on Butler and in chatting with him suggested that he rewrite his *Press* articles.[1] Butler did this work on Sundays and holidays, while keeping up his painting as his main occupation. Early in 1871 he had nearly finished *Erewhon*.

Sometime before beginning this work he had formed a friendship with Miss Eliza Mary Ann Savage, whom he met at Heatherley's Art School. She had not liked him at first; but one day, when she met him on the street, he silently offered her some cherries from a basket out of which he was eating. She helped herself and went on her way rejoicing, also without a word; she now perceived that he was "different from anyone else."[2] Shortly they began to see more of each other, to exchange ideas, and to write letters which Butler carefully preserved. These letters provide an interesting record of Butler's life up to 1885, the year of Miss Savage's death; and they were not only used by Jones in his biography but later published.[3]

Beginning with *Erewhon*, Miss Savage read the manuscript of each of Butler's books, helping him with her intelligent comments and her unfailing enthusiasm for what he did.[4] The degree of her influence upon him will never be precisely known, but it is evident from the spriteliness of her many communications that she urged him in the direction of wit and satire—her own special bent. Butler feared that she wanted him to marry her, which he was not prepared to do; she, on the other hand, seems to have been happy enough with the friendship he offered and to have desired nothing more.[5]

Butler sent the manuscript of *Erewhon* to the publishing house of Chapman and Hall which, on the advice of its reader, George Meredith, rejected it. Butler's characteristic comment about this rejection was that it was not strange; he would have rejected Meredith's work if it had been submitted to him. Although Trübner published *Erewhon* in 1872, it was not at the firm's own risk.[6] However, it was a success, not only because the unsigned first edition was thought to be by Lord Lytton,[7] but also because of its merits. It was the only book by Butler which brought him a profit, and nine editions were printed during his lifetime; eight were with minor revisions, but the ninth contained considerable rewriting and many additions. A commonplace of Butler criticism has been to state that all his major ideas are to be found in *Erewhon*—but this statement is accurate only because he put them into the 1901 revision.[8] The 1872 edition gives, therefore, a better picture of the state of his thoughts at that time. In the discussion which follows, references are to the first edition when its wording differs from that of the 1901 text.

II *Into a New World*

The hero of *Erewhon* remains nameless until in *Erewhon Revisited* he is called Higgs. He is a hired hand on a sheep range in an unidentified country where he goes exploring with the hope of finding wealth and fame. A simpleminded egotist with no awareness of the contradictions in his own nature, he states that his aim is to make money out of the Erewhonians by selling them as cheap labor to the colonists. Then he adds: "I have a very genuine dislike for all unhandsome dealings in money matters" (59). He tells us that he catechized the native Chowbok who is his guide on the trip he is taking and explained to him the mysteries of original sin, "with which I was myself familiar, having been the grandson of an archdeacon" (28). He says his prayers and observes Sundays faithfully.

Still, the opening chapters of the story present tellingly the

psychology of transformation in symbolic terms—the transition
from a world where things we understand are in their places to
the new realm of Erewhon where the ground rules are changed.
Before the trip starts, in a woodshed, said to be like a cathedral
and with one votive candle burning in it, Higgs gets his first ink-
ling of what may lie ahead for him as he watches Chowbok sitting statuelike on the bales of wool and grimacing frightfully.
Once the trip has started, there are two treacherous valleys to
cross, and Higgs must lose his guide and go on alone before he
can assail the second valley. It is by mere chance that he goes onward, for the clouds open only momentarily to reveal "a glimpse
of an immeasurable extent of blue and distant plains" (20).
Chance dominates life, and we must be there to seize the magic
moment because it may not come again: "Had I arrived five min-
utes later, the cloud would have been over the pass, and I should
not have known of its existence."

As he goes down the cliff Higgs becomes so horrified by the
strangeness of his surroundings that he momentarily loses his
head. Later, when he camps in the ravine, he realizes that he cannot return. "It is a dreadful feeling that of being cut off from all
one's kind. . . . I do not believe that any man could long retain
his reason in such solitude. . . . One begins doubting one's own
identity" (23). During the night he dreams of a gigantic organ
thundering "arpeggioed harmonics" on the mountainside, and a
voice says "It is Handel"—the man whom Butler had most worshiped since his early youth thus accompanies Higgs as he crosses
his frightening boundary (24).

When Higgs awakes, he hears the ghostly sound the wind
makes blowing through the ten statues at the pass into Erewhon
—the Ten Commandments of Christianity which by formalizing
our lives, Butler suggests, have kept us from coming nearer to
ourselves. We must pass these and leave them behind; we ought
not to be frightened by them since they are really only hollow
bogeymen. "I had a far worse time of it than I have told [the
reader] and I strongly recommend him to remain in Europe if
he can" (25); that is, remain in the realm of accepted thoughts.
Crossing the turbulent river, Higgs again loses control and is almost drowned; he tells us that he cannot "remember anything at
all save flying over furious waters." When he reaches the opposite bank, he says, "How I got there I do not know" (1872 ed.).

Finally he ascends to the pass into Erewhon and sees the ten stone statues. "I believe I fainted," he says, "for how long I shall never know. I was deadly sick and cold when I came to myself. . . . I am afraid I cried out. I felt sure that I could never get back alive" (1872 ed.).

These details deserve notice because they suggest a symbolic treatment of Butler's own movement out of the convictions of his youth and his era and that the change, not merely intellectual but also spiritual, was a traumatic experience. The emotional overtones are all too clear. The journey is a frightening one into the reversals of unconscious perception. Later Higgs is able to laugh at the trick the statues played on him (38). Once across the pass, man can come, at least in part, to himself.

III *The Story Unfolds*

The plot of *Erewhon* is briefly as follows. Soon after his arrival in the new country the hero is taken captive and is treated with kindness by Yram, the jailkeeper's daughter, with whom he falls in love. Later he is forced to leave her and is conveyed to the capital city where he lives with a wealthy banker, Mr. Nosnibor. The major part of the book is devoted to an account of his adventures in the capital as he gradually becomes acquainted with the ways of its inhabitants. He develops a strong affection for Arowhena, Mr. Nosnibor's daughter, whom he persuades to elope with him. Under pretext of conducting a scientific experiment, he receives financial aid from the queen to build a balloon. When he discovers that an enemy faction at court is planning to bring him to trial for possessing a watch, he decides, just in time, to make his escape in the balloon, although it is not ready for flight. He and Arowhena float away and when the balloon finally loses its buoyancy and descends into the ocean, they are rescued by an Italian vessel and returned to Europe.

In spite of the opening of this romance, which suggests a voyage into an ideal world, Erewhon is no utopia; many things are changed, yet the Erewhonians are as embedded in their own absurdities as the Victorians were in theirs. Butler could not make a complete break. His imagination throws light on things that *are,* as does the imagination of Lewis Carroll in the world of *Alice in Wonderland.* His world is "over the range" rather than "down a rabbit hole." It comes to grips with very real problems and suggests prophetic thoughts. But it does not sweep us onward toward a glorious resolution. Rather, Butler seems to say that the unconscious is not a happy place.

Erewhon offers no easy escape. The value it has rests in its capacity to clarify our relations with the world in which we must live as best we can. It anticipates and exercises the same kind of power as did the findings of later anthropologists and sociologists about the relativity of ethical codes and human behavior; these findings frightened people when, during the decades ahead, the specialists carried out investigations into the relativity of moral values, just such investigations as are implicit in Butler's imaginative work. No wonder then that the journey to Erewhon is fraught with difficulty. In spite of the fun and laughter, danger lurks. The theme of breakdown is in the background. After his second visit to Erewhon, in *Erewhon Revisited*, Higgs suffers a complete mental collapse, as does also John Pickard Owen, the central figure of *The Fair Haven*, after his attempt to grapple with the enigma of the Christian miracles.

IV   *Erewhonian Morality*

The first glimpses of the country of Erewhon bring relief and happiness. While the description of the pass itself is of the New Zealand mountains, the landscape of Erewhon is that of northern Italy, Butler's heavenly kingdom. The radiant healthiness of the inhabitants is extraordinary because, as we later learn, they regard illness as a crime. Also they have banned machines, taking their clue from a philosopher who argues much as Butler had argued in "Darwin among the Machines."

The Erewhonians reverse the European code; to them moral delinquency is a disease, calling not for social disapprobation but for sympathy and the expert treatment of a "straightener," who operates much as a modern psychoanalyst. Senoj Nosnibor (Robinson Jones), the wealthy banker with whom our hero stays, has "embezzled a large sum of money under singularly distressing circumstances" from a helpless widow (who, in the 1901 revision, would have been prosecuted for misplaced confidence if she had not died) and is having long sessions with his straightener who is curing him of his unfortunate propensities.

Still, there is no real perfection in Erewhon. People cheat as in Europe, feigning moral delinquency to cover physical ailments,

rather than vice versa. "To have the socks" (1901 addition, 74)—
that is, to have stolen a pair of socks—is a recognized way of
saying that one is indisposed. The brutal treatment meted out to
sufferers from minor sicknesses is as shocking as our worst penal
practices; yet the people are healthy on the whole, and the
wicked system seems to work. The vigorous summary speech by
the judge who is condemning a pneumonia victim to life im-
prisonment in the chapter "Some Erewhonian Trials" was taken
by Butler from a newspaper report of a judge's summary in an
English court. He merely substituted "consumption" for "theft." [9]
But the Erewhonians, like nineteenth-century Englishmen, are
moving toward reform; there is secret practice of medicine and a
growing conviction that the courts are too harsh. The reformers
would continue to flog and hang, but they would do so with pity.

V *Erewhonian Religion*

The "Musical Banks" at which the Erewhonians worship are
used to express Butler's criticism of ethical dualism and of religious hypocrisy. While really worshiping the goddess Ydgrun
(Grundy), the Erewhonians set great store by their public at-
tendance at the Musical Banks in which they deposit a special
form of currency that has no practical value whatsoever. Even
the ministers of the church, the least agreeable people in Erewhon, are insulted if anyone seeks to pay them with their own
worthless coin. But the Musical Bank buildings, old and vener-
able, and the pompous ceremonies impress the hero; they lead
him to the conclusion that, in spite of the apparently ridiculous
nature of the whole operation, it must embody some deep traditional wisdom. The point of the satire is made clear when Butler
tells us that "The Musical Banks paid little or no dividend, but
divided their profits by way of bonus on the original shares once
in every thirty thousand years; and as it was now only two thousand years since there had been one of these distributions, people felt that they could not hope for another in their own time
and preferred investments whereby they got some more tangible
return" (113). The care with which Butler had to cover his tracks
is shown by the 1872 edition's reading three hundred and fifty
and two hundred years, respectively, thus robbing the passage
of its obvious point by removing the reference to the birth of
Christ.

The Erewhonians insist upon personifying everything they regard as admirable or anything they do not understand. Our hero reasons with Arowhena, by arguing that personification does not explain the operation of the ideal nor of that which is not understood. Later, when he has explained his own religion to her, she turns his argument back upon him, criticizing his conception of God. She says "that people would no more cease to love God on ceasing to believe in His objective personality, than they had ceased to love justice on discovering that she was not really personal; nay, that they would never truly love Him till they saw Him thus" (127). In the 1901 edition Butler added the following passage, which expresses his final faith as well as anything else he wrote:

Nevertheless, her remarks have haunted me, and I have since met with many very godly people who have had a great knowledge of divinity, but no sense of the divine: and again, I have seen a radiance upon the face of those who were worshipping the divine either in art or nature—in picture or statue—in field or cloud or sea—in man, woman, or child —which I have never seen kindled by any talking about the nature and attributes of God. Mention but the word divinity, and our sense of the divine is clouded.   (128)

In another chapter, Butler enlarges his discussion of Ydgrun. In it his desire to judge men for what they are, not for what they pretend to be, emerges most strongly. He is actually praising the well-rounded Englishman of his day:

They [the Ydgrunites] were gentlemen in the full sense of the word; and what has one not said in saying this? . . . Being strong, and handsome, and kindly nurtured, moreover being inured from youth to exercises and athletics of all sorts, and living fearlessly under the eye of their peers, among whom there exists a high standard of courage, generosity, honour, and every good and manly quality—what wonder that they should have become, so to speak, a law unto themselves; and, while taking an elevated view of the goddess Ydgrun, they should have gradually lost all faith in the recognized deities of their country? . . . The example of a real gentleman is, if I may say so without profanity, the best of all gospels.   (130-32, with addition from 1872 ed.)

Yet Higgs desires to convert even these ideal men and to save them from "their certain ultimate perdition."

The Erewhonians regard the doctrine of immortality as immoral because it would lead people to think this life of secondary importance. But they have a mythology of preexistence, and they profess to believe that it is the pestering of the unborn which causes parents to have children. The birth formula to which all children must subscribe exonerates their parents from any blame in their birth. The child vows that "he did with malice aforethought set himself to plague and pester two unfortunate people who had never wronged him, and who were quite contented and happy until he conceived this base design against their peace; for which wrong he now humbly entreats their pardon" (137). This mythology of the unborn describes the suffering both to parents and to the children caused by mismatches decreed by fate; it also warns the would-be infant of the certainty of death, of the burden of free will, and of the miseries of life which those who desire to leave the realm of the unborn will bring upon themselves. The only consolation for one who has unwisely chosen to be born is that, if he will do his "present and immediate duty" each day of his life, he may safely get through the trials that lie ahead of him.

VI *Erewhonian Education*

Having broached the subject of parents and children, Butler cannot refrain from discussing education. The Erewhonians, like their European mirror images, have an absurd educational system in their "Colleges of Unreason," one aim of which is to incapacitate young people so that they will be unable to lead useful lives; but the Erewhonians are far more conscious of what they are doing than Europeans are. Mr. Thims, who takes Higgs through the university, explains that the students are drilled in "hypothetics," which enlarges their horizons by presenting them with "a set of utterly strange and impossible contingencies" (162). The students are taught a synthetic language of no conceivable use, and they are drilled in the principles of "unreason" on the premise that "there is hardly an error into which men may not easily be led if they base their conduct upon reason only" (164). Although the buildings at the university are so beautiful as to have "a hallowing and refining influence which is in itself half an education" (170), the professors "seemed to devote themselves to the avoidance of every opinion with which they were not perfectly familiar, and regarded their brains as a sort of sanctuary, to which if an opinion had once resorted, none other was to attack it" (170).

VII   *Attack on Machines*

At the university Higgs discusses the revolt against the machines with a learned professor of antiquities. He is given "The Book of the Machines" which presents the entire story. This part of *Erewhon* reminds the reader of Carlyle's *Sartor Resartus:* There is an elaborate mystification about omitted passages, editorial changes, apologies and explanations, as though Butler, like Carlyle, had to stand at a distance from his material to insure his control of it. The reasoning presented to show that machines may indeed be the next stage in evolutionary development is more compelling and detailed than in Butler's early articles on this subject. After citing numerous analogies between the behavior of living organisms and the behavior of machines, the Erewhonian writer asks "Whether strictly speaking we should not ask what kind of levers a man is made of rather than what is his temperament?" (179). Then, Butler has Higgs tell us, the author "became more and more obscure, so that I was obliged to give up all attempt at translation" (179).

Higgs again essays translation, and he gives a passage in which the Erewhonian savant points out that such organs as the eye and the brain serve the individual much as machines do—they are comparable to microscopes, telescopes, or mechanical computers. Then suddenly he views the body as a whole congeries of machines: "Our blood is composed of infinite living agents which go up and down the highways and byways of our bodies as people in the streets of a city" (183). Once more our hero interposes: "Here the writer became again so hopelessly obscure that I was obliged to miss several pages" (183).

"The Book of the Machines" resumes by warning that, although it is now impossible to do away with all machines, their development must be stopped if they are to be prevented from winning mastery over mankind: "How many men at this hour are living in a state of bondage to the machines?" (185). "Consider . . . the colliers and pitmen and coal merchants and coal trains, and the men who drive them, and the ships that carry coals—what an army of servants do the machines thus employ! Are there not probably more men engaged in tending machinery than in tending men?" (186). The Erewhonian savant discusses the objection to his line of reasoning which says that machines are not organic because they cannot reproduce themselves, and he counters by asking how many "machines are there which have not been produced systematically by other machines?" (188). If it is replied that man makes them do so, the answer is that there are "whole families of plants [which would] die out if their fertilization were not effected by a class of agents utterly foreign to themselves" (188). The argument that a thimble cannot make another thimble is met by pointing out that "very few creatures reproduce after their own kind." Thus "the butterfly lays an egg, which egg can become a caterpillar, which caterpillar can become a chrysalis, which chrysalis can become a butterfly" (189).

A little later in the argument Higgs again finds "a very long and untranslatable digression" (192) about the different races and families of machines. This is followed by a discussion of free will, which culminates in the conclusion that man is really no freer than the machine. Finally the point is made that we have come to depend on machines ourselves so that "it is the machines which act upon man and make him man, as much as man who has acted upon and made the machines" (199). To prevent a dishonorable future of slavery, we must destroy these machines now, no matter at what cost to ourselves; we must not give in to those who argue that slavery is better than death. Thus revolution is decreed. What would the Erewhonians say of our atomic bomb—the ultimate of all machines?

At this point in his presentation Higgs builds his balloon and escapes from Erewhon with Arowhena, hearing in the mist over the ocean "the last few bars of the first part of the minuet in Saul" (1872 ed.). Thus his guardian angel Handel, whose organ playing he had heard as he entered the country, is with him again as he leaves.

VIII *What Does It Mean?*

We now have before us the working out of a whole set of iconoclastic notions. That Butler was serious about this material is indicated by a comment he made in 1900 in reference to *Erewhon:* "I . . . was surprised (and, I may add, shocked) that anyone could doubt my having been serious—very much so—in my own way." [10] Why then did he make his book a fantasy? Was it because it took more daring than he possessed at the time to face up to the total implications of his views? Was it because he wished to avoid shocking his readers more than they could stand, which, if he did, would prevent any kind of a hearing? Or was it simply that the notions came to him in this form and had to be so expressed—to protect both himself and his readers? Certain it is that if the Erewhonian mood should become too extreme in anyone, allowing him to question every human relation, alienation might result. Who knows how much of this mood we can take and still preserve the strength to aspire to the state of the High Ydgrunites, those self-confident, noble compromisers and men of the world whom Butler admired most of all? The phrase "in my own way" is the key phrase in Butler's statement. Some deep impulse had said to him: Go thus far and no further. Perhaps he went too far for many of his readers whose defense reaction is to find his work ridiculous—the safety valve he himself provided—but for others this book acts as a genuine revelation of new possibilities.

From the start, *Erewhon* was criticized not in terms of what it is but in terms of what critics thought it should be. *The Academy* for August 1, 1872, found the novel's narrative lacking in sustained power; its satire inconsistent, since not all the features of European society are shown in reverse; and its attempt to portray an ideal society a failure because the Erewhonians are not ideal—if they were, they would not punish their sick. The reviewer called *Erewhon* "a dull book throughout." *The Athenaeum*[11] also called it "slovenly" because of its inconsistencies, complained of its attack on Darwinism, and recommended that its author return to sheep farming and give up writing altogether. The *British Quarterly Review*[12] expressed bewilderment: "The effect of the whole is disappointing, where it is not unintelligible . . . we are utterly at a loss to see the relevance or meaning of many of the illustrations selected. Either they are simply unmeaning or absolutely foolish." *The Fortnightly Review*[13] called the book the work of a beginner which could easily have been made better if the author had taken pains with it. It has "plenty of good points in detail, but no particular point on the whole." The *Saturday Review*,[14] which objected to the immorality of the treatment of vice and virtue, called *Erewhon* too farfetched and complicated. The *Spectator*[15] praised it as the ablest book of its sort since Swift, but called its author a "universal sceptic" who was opposed to all abstract thought, all religion, all principles of morality. Those who take its teaching seriously, the reviewer said, will find themselves in Erewhon—nowhere—when they have done.

These samples of the critical remarks, which constitute the best "press" Butler received during his lifetime, indicate clearly what he confronted in doing the kind of work he wanted to do—and how careful he would have to be if he aspired to favorable attention. As he came to realize, originality is always puzzling to the guardians of the *status quo*. This realization caused Butler in his 1901 revision of *Erewhon* to include some comments on originality: "genius was like offences—needs must that it come, but woe unto that man through whom it comes. A man's business, they hold, is to think as his neighbors do" (165). Butler slowly discovered that, if he were to have an audience at all, it would be a future audience. At the same time he continued to do everything he could, short of compromising himself, to win readers; and the amount of review space that was given to his books is actually somewhat surprising. A lone wolf, paying his way with his publishers, would not fare so well in the 1960's as Butler did nearly a century ago.

Butler feared that his "Book of the Machines" would distress Charles Darwin. Two months after *Erewhon* appeared, he wrote Darwin to say that he had developed these ideas "for mere fun . . . without a particle of serious meaning" and that he had aimed his satire at Bishop Butler's *Analogy of Religion* but had not dared to make this clear in his book.[16] In the preface to the second edition (June, 1872) he said that "nothing could be further from my intention . . . than any attempt to laugh at Mr. Darwin" (xix). The subsequent direction of Butler's work certainly raises a question as to whether, when he made these comments, he really understood his own intention. Was he simply being diplomatic, or was he being true only to a superficial awareness of himself? He later said that no author in the flush of a first success is to be trusted with the writing of a preface. But the immediate result was that Darwin invited him to his home for a weekend, the first of the two visits Butler paid him.

CHAPTER 3

Pro and Contra

I *Another Satire*

AFTER the publication of *Erewhon*, Miss Savage urged Butler to write a full-fledged novel. He considered several possible plots involving satiric treatment of sectarianism, but rejected them all because he feared he might use them merely as pegs on which to hang his ideas.[1] Instead, he set to work on another project of elaborate mystification, putting the substance of his 1865 pamphlet on the Resurrection into a complex framework calculated to entrap the wariest reader and, perhaps, even himself. *The Fair Haven*, a vivid fictional restatement of the development of his own thoughts about Christianity, was published in 1873.

The method Butler used was to interpose two imaginary authors—John Pickard Owen and William Bickersteth Owen—between himself and this material with so many protestations of its meaning the opposite of what it evidently did mean that most readers would hardly know what he was getting at. This is a clever satiric trick to play, and there is abundant evidence from his letters and notes to prove that Butler was playing it on purpose;[2] but it is played so very cleverly and the argument is so complex that the reader cannot help thinking that Butler protests too much. Again, the dramatic form he adopts indicates a genuine ambiguity in his feelings toward what he is doing, in spite of all he said to his friends to the contrary and even in spite of his preface to the second edition in which he ostensibly laid his cards on the table.

The "Memoir of the Late John Pickard Owen," which opens *The Fair Haven*, is the most effective section of the volume. Really a novel in miniature, it presents several living characters. In its recounting of John's life from infancy, it describes his childhood pranks, his inquisitive mind, and the influence on him of his father and mother. He is an industrious student, acquiring a knowledge of Latin and Greek and scrutinizing all his beliefs with careful logic. The first real shock to his faith comes when, as a Sunday School teacher at the age of seventeen, he discovers no correlation among his students between those who are good and those who are bad, and those who have been baptized and those who have not. At first he convinces himself that baptism as performed in the established church must be ineffectual, so he joins the Baptists, but soon he quarrels with them over their doctrine of predestination. Next he becomes a Roman Catholic, but he soon rebels against the stifling of free inquiry. Then he adopts the Deistic point of view. After years of meditation and study, during which he does the writing which forms the body of *The Fair Haven* and passes through all the phases of skepticism and doubt, he arrives at what is essentially a Broad Church position. Unfortunately, at this time his overworked brain gives way, he relapses into a profound religious melancholy, and dies.

II *Exercise in Ambiguity*

We are made aware early in the "Memoir" of the genuine shock to John, a sincere and clear-thinking youngster, when he discovers that life is not what it pretends to be: that women are not "all solid woman" (6) but have legs beneath their elaborate skirts and petticoats; that chicken and sheep are not solid meat as they should be but are "mere skin and bone covering a cavern" (7); and that grown-ups are not above saying their prayers when children are watching but not saying them when they think they are unobserved (10). What a shock to discover that the world is a bundle of pretenses! Further, what a shock to discover that one's conception of God is modeled on one's conception of one's father (8), and that Evangelical literalism is "the main obstacle to the complete overthrow of unbelief"! (3). And finally, what a shock to the reader to discover that *The Fair Haven* is not sincere, but a satire, and then to find that it is not a satire, but sincere!

Mrs. Owen's daydreams of her sons as Christian martyrs and of herself as the elect of God reveal a genuinely disagreeable character, although John's brother, William Bickersteth Owen, never tires of protesting his devotion to her. Her literal faith in the Bible and her respect for honesty and booklearning set her son John an impossible goal which forces him, because of the unrelenting rigor of his mind, "to give up not only his mother but

Christ Himself for Christ's sake" (15). After John discovers that baptism has no discernible effect on the characters of those baptized and he passes through his various religious phases, William comments that John's mental anguish resulted directly from his never having been taught to see more than one side of a question —as the youthful Butler had never been taught. When, years later, John wins through beyond his Deism to genuine broadmindedness, he looks upon young people who already have mental freedom and remarks: "With a great sum obtained I this freedom; but thou wast free-born" (19). Yet, adds William, John gained something from his suffering: "Awakening to the perception of the whole after an intimate acquaintance with the details, he was able to realize the position and meaning of all that he had hitherto experienced in a way which has been vouchsafed to few, if any others. . . . He was as one who has made the circuit of a mountain, and yet been ascending during the whole time of his doing so: such a person finds himself upon the same side as at first, but upon a greatly higher level" (20-21).

III *Real Faith?*

John Pickard Owen's great discovery, which emerges from the mental anguish he endures, is that the discrepancies and inconsistencies he finds in the Bible strengthen rather than weaken faith, "inasmuch as the true spiritual conception in the mind of man could be indirectly more certainly engendered by a strife, a warring, a clashing, so to speak, of versions, all of them distorting slightly some one or other of the features of the original, than directly by the most absolutely correct impression which human language could convey" (22). Again, satire apart, is this not close to the pragmatic view of truth Butler himself was later to defend so strongly? And is this not also close to the aims of his satiric method?

Yet Butler is indeed making fun of John Pickard Owen, and thus also of himself. The skill with which he traces the inconsistencies in the Gospels—for this is his central topic—is only equaled by the sanctimonious glibness with which he justifies the inconsistencies by attributing them to divine will and wisdom. He imitates to perfection the high-flown, self-satisfied rhetoric of the higher criticism; and the whole argument becomes a travesty of right reason, since it assumes the very thing the miracles are supposed to prove—namely, the truth of the Christian story. Armed with his preposterous theory, John finds that the very arguments which lead so many to atheism become for him the "foundation-stone of faith." He is a veritable Don Quixote of religion, like Philip H. Gosse who convinced himself that fossil remains had been planted in the earth to test man's faith.[3] The overpious tone of the work certainly makes its point, yet the reader must still beware of rejecting too much. He should remember that the preface to the second edition in which Butler holds up to scorn the unfortunate reviewers who took his first edition seriously may very well be just another turn of the screw. Perhaps, after all, Butler did mean something serious by his elaborate and carefully reasoned hoax.

IV *Attack on Reason*

Actually, *The Fair Haven* is a virtuoso attack on human reason, using the theological arguments so dear to the Victorians but calculated to make the head of any careful reader spin. Filled with analogies drawn from painting and music and science, it probes again and again at the basis of the rational process and comes close to suggesting that the mind cannot arrive at any truth at all. It is a highly artistic, controlled presentation of the mental anguish that had tormented the author himself for fourteen years; it is also an early example of the sort of exploration of the logical processes which was to be carried further by later psychological and philosophical writers. How William James would have enjoyed it! [4]

William Bickersteth Owen tells us that John was delighted to find that Dean Alford not only admitted an irreconcilable conflict between the Gospels of St. Luke and St. Matthew but also said that he believed them both (26). John contends that Dean Alford, without being fully aware of it, was right in realizing that "the spiritual value of each account was no less precious for not being in strict accordance with the other," and that what counts is "the subjective truth conveyed by both the narratives, which lives in our hearts independently of precise knowledge concerning the actual facts" (27). Who can say that there is no truth in this view? But what problems it creates for conscious reason!

If we are men of moods and if we also wish to be true to ourselves, how can we expect to be consistent and rational? Should

[51]

rationality and consistency take precedence over personal integrity and happiness? Or are the former qualities inventions of a puritanical conscientiousness designed to generate nothing but unhappiness? What is reality? This is a question that the nineteenth century kept asking. Its probing culminated in F. H. Bradley's *Appearance and Reality,* the final statement of absolute idealism, in which all contradictions merge. Butler, in a nonacademic fashion, was on a similar path. Thus John Pickard Owen was "alternately under the influence of two conflicting spirits—at one time writing as though there were nothing precious under the sun except logic . . . at another leading the reader almost to believe that he disregarded the value of any objective truth. . . . Whenever he was in one mood he seemed to forget the possibility of any other" (29). We can smile at this situation, as Butler intended that we should; but it may also give us pause for thought. It is in part Butler's evaluation in 1873 of the state of mind which eight years earlier had led him to write his Resurrection pamphlet; in part, it is his attempt to put the material of this pamphlet into a satiric setting to force those who had neglected his ideas then to attend to them now.

V *Subversive Doctrine*

One section of the "Memoir" presents a group of quotations from John's commonplace book, written before he regained his faith. Many of the ideas developed in the quotations appear in the notes Butler began to collect a few years after the appearance of *The Fair Haven.* For example, in March, 1883, Butler wrote: "The Song of Solomon and the book of Esther are the most interesting in the Old Testament, but these are the very ones that make the smallest pretensions to holiness, and even these are neither of them of very transcendent merit. . . . Ecclesiastes contains some fine things but is strongly tinged with pessimism, cynicism, and affectation . . . . the Psalms generally are poor and, for the most part, querulous, spiteful, and introspective into the bargain . . ." (*Note-Books,* 201). John Pickard Owen likewise complains, "The parables which every one praises are in reality very bad: The Unjust Steward, the Labourers in the Vineyard, the Prodigal Son, Dives and Lazarus, the Sower and the Seed . . . are all either grossly immoral, or tend to engender a very low estimate of the character of God" (*The Fair Haven,* 39).

And he adds, "The value of generosity and magnanimity was perfectly well known among the ancients, nor do these qualities assume any nobler guise in the teaching of Christ than they did in that of the ancient heathen philosophers" (39). He then states that the Christian emphasis on self-denial is a poor substitute for "generosity and high spirit" (40), and he questions whether Christianity has done anything at all to contribute to the spread of these qualities: "The ideal presented by the character of Christ . . . offers but a peevish view of life and things in comparison with that offered by other highest ideals—the old Roman and Greek ideals, the Italian ideal, and the Shakespearean ideal" (41).

Of course Butler hoped that by planting subversive doctrine of this sort in a book ostensibly defending the miraculous element in Christianity some of it might stick. In this section he presents also an eloquent plea for honesty to oneself: "What can we feel towards one who for a small motive tells lies even to himself, and does not know that he is lying? . . . The common self-deceiver of modern society is a more dangerous and contemptible object than almost any ordinary felon" (43). Here we may ask: If a man lies to himself and does not know that he is lying, who or what is to tell him? And why is it a lie unless he has a larger self than he is aware of? Butler, obviously, is appealing to this larger self rather than saying: "I know better what you should believe than you do."

John finally attacks Christianity directly: "It is only conventional Christianity which will stand a man in good stead to live by; true Christianity will never do so. . . . And what if some unhappy wretch, with a serious turn of mind and no sense of the ridiculous, takes all this talk about Christianity in sober earnest, and tries to act on it? Into what misery may he not easily fall, and with what life-long errors may he not embitter the lives of his children!" (44-45). On all of this, his brother William comments: "His mind was indeed in darkness!" (46).

VI *The Negative Argument*

After this introductory material comes John Pickard Owen's account of the growth of infidelity in his day. He tells us that the reasoning of Bishop Butler and of Paley is no longer convincing in his era, and he explains that only he who fully understands the position of the faithless man will be able to win him back to faith—his arguments must be comprehended before they can be refuted. He then embarks on a long and detailed statement of the reasons the faithless man has for rejecting the miracle of the Resurrection, remarking at frequent intervals that he is reserving his answering argument, calculated to demolish his position, until the end. First he elaborately refutes the "hallucination theory" of Strauss, arguing that since the ardent faith of the Apostles arose as a result of the Resurrection, it cannot be reckoned a cause of the Apostles' thinking that they saw Christ alive when they really did not. This part of the essay is effective. It has all the appearance of something Butler really did believe in and is an excellent example of his powers in cogent analysis.

Having silenced Strauss, our amateur theologian next takes up the issue of the discrepancies among the various Gospel accounts of the Resurrection. Again the argument is acute and vigorous. He draws on "an anonymous pamphlet" of 1865 (Butler's own) and subjects the Gospel accounts, Dean Alford's notes, and the German commentators to minute scrutiny. His constant plea is that we face up to the facts, and his chief delight is to point out that no one so far has done so. The acuteness of his reasoning about such a matter as the wound in the Saviour's side and Dean Alford's "disgraceful" notes on it reminds us of the perverted ingenuity of Dostoevsky's Smerdyakov. There is no good reply to be made to this probing analysis, any more than there is to Smerdyakov's, but we are amazed at the mind of one who can indulge in it. No wonder theologians of his day preferred to leave this skillful swordsman alone! No wonder Butler was annoyed that no opponent would fight with him! John Owen's conclusion at this point is: "We have no proof of His [Christ's] having died at all!" (152).

John likens Dean Alford to "a disreputable attorney," but then he shifts the blame onto theologians in general: "One would have thought he [Dean Alford] could have been guilty of nothing short of infatuation in hoping that the above notes would pass muster with any ordinarily intelligent person . . . [but] his confidence has not been misplaced. Of all those engaged in the training of our young men for Holy Orders . . . whose very profession it is to be lovers of truth and candour . . . *not a single one,* so far as I know, has raised his voice in protest. If a man has not lost his power of weeping, let him weep for this" (153-54). "No truthful mind can doubt," he concludes, "that the cause of Christ is far better served by exposing an insufficient argument than by silently passing it over" (154). Here again it seems evident that Butler means what he has John Pickard Owen say.

VII *Is There an Answer?*

At this point John again reminds us, so that we may not "be swallowed up in overmuch grief at the journey" yet before us, that eventually we may "let the wings of our soul expand" in full and certain faith (157). But he agrees with the man who is unfaithful that "a certain amount of care should be taken before the credentials [of the Apostles] are accepted" (165), and he presents in the unfaithful man's words a detailed analysis of the exact discrepancies in the Gospel accounts of the scene at the tomb. So carefully does he do so that the reader emerges wondering how anyone could ever have accepted such inconsistent versions. The conclusion that the unfaithful man finally reaches is "that Jesus Christ really did reappear shortly after the Crucifixion, and that his reappearance, though due to natural causes, was conceived to be miraculous" (186). John Pickard Owen at this point concedes that "the unhappy man whose views I have been endeavouring to represent above" (187) is correct in regarding St. Matthew's account as unreliable, and that our Lord never foretold his Resurrection. "We have now seen," the doubt-ridden man then concludes, "that there is no evidence worth the name, for any miracle in connection with the tomb of Christ" (190). At this point, John says that, before he undertakes to show the "futility and irrelevancy" of the unfaithful one's reasoning, he will allow him a few more words. In these few words, the unfaithful man examines the evidence for the Ascension and rejects it.

At last we have come to the long-awaited counterattack. "I have completed a task painful to myself and to the reader," John tells us, "painful to myself inasmuch as I am humiliated upon remembering the power which arguments, so shallow and so easily to be refuted, once had upon me; painful to the reader, as everything must be painful which even appears to throw doubt upon the most sublime event that has happened in human history" (209). He now plays his trump card: "The incomparable *chiaroscuro* of the Evangelistic writings" (216) is the very element which has given universality to the Christ-ideal. "It is not what a man has actually put upon his canvas, but what he makes us feel that he felt, which makes the difference between good and bad. . . . Do we not detect an analogy to this in the records of the Evangelists? . . . We can see *through* these things as through a glass darkly. . . . We may indeed see less of the actual lineaments themselves, but the echo is ever more spiritually tuneful than the sound, and the echo we find within us" (216-17).

John's argument then is that "all ideals gain by vagueness and lose by definition" (220); he contends that the Gospels have "the error distributed skilfully among them, as in a well-tuned instrument" (223), and precisely in the order required to create this necessary vagueness. To buttress his theory, he cites as evidence of its truth the century-long appeal of the Resurrection story to millions of men. "The bare contemplation of such a stupendous misapplication of self-sacrifice and energy [if Christianity is based on fallacy] should be enough to prevent any one from ever smiling again to whose mind such a deplorable view was present" (239). In conclusion, John extols the "candour" "that has taken us safely into the Fair Haven of universal brotherhood in Christ" (246).

VIII *Satire or Not?*

The strange thing about the conclusion to *The Fair Haven*, if viewed as the satire which in many of its details it assuredly is, is that Butler himself through the rest of his life never ceased to explore the possibility of seeing truth in the terms he had set forth here—not in logical isolation or as a thing in itself, but as a give-and-take of forces and as something which relates to the accumulated wisdom of mankind. So, in spite of the sanctimonious tone of John's argument and in spite of the fact that he never meets the unfaithful on his own grounds—as he had all along promised to do—he speaks in Butler's voice. It is satire, but what a many-voiced satire it is! *The Fair Haven* explores an internal debate that ends with the issues unresolved. It is dramatic, and it lives for us today if we can understand that the issues presented are matters of life or death. All this is true even though John Pickard Owen lapses into "a religious melancholy which nothing could disturb" and dies "in a state little better than idiocy" (56), and it is true even though Butler included in *The Fair Haven* a chapter on "The Christ-Ideal" so platitudinous that he himself characterized it as "the kind of rubbish that would go down with the *Spectator*." [5]

Butler hoped that his book would be attacked. He then would have, he said, "an opportunity for excusing myself; and, if so, I shall endeavour that the excuse may be worse than the fault it is intended to excuse." [6] But no attack of this sort was forthcoming, though *The Academy* condemned the book as an immoral performance, just as it had condemned *Erewhon*.[7] *The Rock* and *The Scotsman* reviewed it as a serious defense of Christianity; the reviewer in *The National Reformer* was puzzled by it; and the author of a pamphlet entitled *Jesus versus Christianity* recognized its satiric purpose (xix-xxi). Charles Darwin, to whom Butler sent a copy, wrote Butler: "It has interested me greatly and is extremely curious. If I had not known that you had written it I should not even have suspected that the author was not orthodox, within the wide stated limits. . . . What has struck me much in your book is your dramatic power . . . the way in which you earnestly and thoroughly assume the character and think the thoughts of the man you pretend to be." [8]

CHAPTER 4

"In Very Serious Earnest"

I The Way of All Flesh *and Financial Crisis*

UNDAUNTED by the financial failure of *The Fair Haven* (it sold only 442 copies up to 1899[1]), Butler immediately began working on the novel which was to become *The Way of All Flesh*. He continued to paint at Heatherley's Art School, and his picture "Mr. Heatherley's Holiday" was exhibited at the Royal Academy in 1874, along with the portrait, "A Child's Head"; but in order to write he gave up the hour in the evening during which he was wont to play the piano. On August 16, 1873, he sent the first fifteen pages of his novel to Miss Savage. She was delighted with it. "If it goes on as it begins, it will be a perfect novel or as nearly so as may be," she wrote.[2] On September 3, Miss Savage reported to Butler that she liked the second chapter even better than the first; on September 9, she commented on chapter five, showing that the work was going ahead rapidly.

Butler, however, could not make up his mind about the narrative method he had adopted—using an observer, Overton, to tell his story. He rewrote some of the early material, dispensing with this observer. Then on November 10, Miss Savage stated her preference for the story as told by a narrator; she said: "I prefer an advocate of flesh and blood," and pointed out that the use of a storyteller would allow naturally for interpretive comment.[3] We can be grateful that she felt this way. On November 24 she discussed Butler's portrait of Alethea with him, though it does not appear that she ever knew that he was drawing a picture of her in this charming, witty character.

By late 1873, work on the novel seems to have slowed down. Butler was having financial troubles which took his attention from his writing. Wishing to keep a closer watch over the investment of his capital with the hope of increasing his income, he recalled from New Zealand the £8,330 to which his capital had now grown and later invested it in a number of companies recommended to him by a banker-friend, Henry Hoare.[4] These investments soon proved the greatest financial error of his life. Instead of prospering, the companies failed; and in the spring of 1874 Henry Hoare failed with them. There was, however, a possibility of retrieving some of the loss if the Canada Tanning Extract Company, of which Butler had been made a director, could be put on its feet. In June he sailed for Canada to see what he could do. During this period of distress, ideas about evolution and machines kept running through his head, and gradually *Life and Habit* shaped itself while the novel waited.

In July he returned briefly to London to report to the board of directors. He was given full power to act, and by August 5, in Montreal once more, he was writing to Miss Savage: "I have fallen among thieves. Well, I believe I may also truly say that the thieves have fallen among *me*." [5] He also told her that he would have to write novels for his bread. "My novel will at last go ahead; but it must be quite innocent . . . I shall have to change the scheme but shall try to keep the earlier chapters." [6] Perhaps Butler soon realized that he could not be "quite innocent." In any case, he does not seem to have gone on with the novel during his stay in Montreal. In May of 1875 he again returned to London for a board meeting, and in December he left Montreal for good. Although he had reduced the company's expenses by £1,600 a year, it could not be saved, and, when final settlement was made, he had remaining to him only £2,000 of his fortune.[7] Now he could no longer live on his income as he had previously done; he had to dip into his capital, which thus gradually diminished.

By 1879 Butler's troubles were so serious that he had to appeal to his father for help. When Butler was still an undergraduate at Cambridge, his family had persuaded him to sign an agreement permitting the sale of the Whitehall mansion and six acres of land. This was a valuable part of an estate left by Butler's grandfather to come to the author by revision on the deaths of his father and aunt who, in the meantime, enjoyed the income from the property but could not sell it without Butler's consent. Butler now felt that he was entitled to something from his father as indemnity for a step he had been persuaded to take when he was too young to know his own rights in the matter. After much discussion, Canon Butler agreed to allow him £300 a year. In

1881, however, the property in question was resettled to give him an absolute revision on which he could borrow, and once this was done his father did not need to give him anything more. Finally, in 1886, when his father died, he inherited the property left him by his grandfather and his financial worries were at an end.

Not until 1878 did Butler resume work on *The Way of All Flesh*. By June 27, he had progressed to Chapter 41, and he hoped to have the novel completed by April, 1879. However, in 1879 he was still busy rewriting parts of it. He worked on the novel again in 1883, and he finally set it aside because he realized that he could not publish it while his father and sisters were alive. He was also in genuine doubt as to its value.[8] Jones tells us that after Miss Savage's death in 1885 Butler did nothing more to the manuscript. It was too closely associated with her in his mind, since she had been the one to encourage his writing it, and he felt a sense of guilt for what he regarded as his egotistical behavior toward her.[9]

II *Genesis of* Life and Habit

Since so many of Butler's ideas about inherited memory are incorporated into *The Way of All Flesh*, it will be well to discuss the four books he wrote from 1878 to 1887 about this subject before examining the novel. As explained earlier, the idea for *Life and Habit* was the outgrowth of Butler's speculations about evolution and machines; it came to him gradually and grew more and more exciting as he worked with it. He had written a key passage about inherited memory in June, 1874, shortly upon his arrival in Montreal (*Unconscious Memory*, 20), but had not grasped the full implications of his own idea at that time. Then in 1876 it assailed him forcefully, and he experienced the excitement and terror of Higgs, the hero of *Erewhon*, as he crosses from one world into another. Although at first he thought the idea might be merely a satiric twist, by February, 1876, he tells us: "I had gripped my meaning, and knew it to be sound."[10] As he worked deeper into the concept of inherited memory, he found: "The theory frightens me—it is so far-reaching and subversive—it oppresses me and I take panics that there cannot really be any solid truth in it . . . do what I can, I am oppressed and frightened."[11] Writing the book literally took his breath away: "I kept wanting to take a long breath, and was quite unable to do so. . . . . It was a full year after *Life and Habit* was published before I righted myself." [12] For the very first time he was truly convinced that he had solved his problem and could lay at rest the doubts and fears that had assailed him since he left for New Zealand. His concern now was how to present his findings effectively so that others could see their validity too.

What Butler was really trying to do was to stem the tide of meaninglessness with which the theory of natural selection was inundating life. He was to become the most dogged, perceptive, and forceful opponent of Darwinism in the nineteenth century; he brought to bear on the underpinnings and implications of the new scientific orthodoxy, as no one else had done, a subtle metaphysical analysis, a kind of classical righteousness of thought, and the full powers of a keen and alert intellect. Unlike the religious fundamentalists of his era, he was not to rely upon authority and accepted tradition for his argument; instead he used the sharp rapier of a practiced mind to reveal that Darwinism did not explain what it pretended to explain. Butler was launched on the quarrel of his life; and he was, as students of the matter now see, to emerge uncompromised and unbowed, for the issues he raised were real ones and abide with us still. Having witnessed the chaos caused in the world by the ruthless application of survival-of-the-fittest doctrine to sociology, politics, and ethics (Hitlerism being a prime example), we are not so ready to laugh at Butler as his age was. Even among biologists, a recent writer tells us: "There will always be a few who feel in their bones a sneaking sympathy with Samuel Butler's scepticism." [13] Basil Willey likewise states: "There have always been a few who have thought, or hoped, that Lamarck and Butler would turn out to be in some sense right after all." [14] In another passage he adds: "It may be that modern genetics and biochemistry will some day discover the mechanism behind the process thus metaphorically described by Lamarck; at any rate, an uneasy feeling has often recurred, in others beside Butler and Shaw, that Lamarck may have been in some sense right after all." [15]

Butler was able to show with a kind of savage glee that the scientific bigwigs of his day, with their philosophical clumsiness and lack of subtlety, constantly smuggled into their arguments the very principles he desired to present forthrightly. He thus brought down upon himself opprobrium, vituperation, and the deadening silence of the "people who are above suspicion." [16] No one believed that the "comic writer" who had produced such puzzling books as *Erewhon* and *The Fair Haven* could have anything serious to say. He had to call up all his resiliency to ride out the storm and to emerge with good humor and calm from a buffeting which assuredly would have sent John Pickard Owen, Higgs, and Ernest Pontifex to the madhouse. Fortunately, Butler understood the risks run by one who assails the citadels of orthodoxy, whether the risks be external or in one's own mind.

III   *The* Life and Habit *Theory*

Butler explored in *Life and Habit* the role of the unconscious as revealed in the uncanny operation of the memory. He noted that the things we know best are the things of which we are least conscious, as exemplified by the accomplished pianist who can play a difficult composition while chatting with a friend. In all of this he was on the same track of investigation as that later pursued by Freud. His aim, though, was not to explore normal or abnormal behavior but to unlock the riddle of evolution. Because he was most interested in ascertaining how individuals travel in the paths of their forefathers without conscious thought about what they are doing, he moved rapidly in the direction of the Jungian archetypes.

Butler's approach is disarmingly simple, and his analysis is full of humor. He says right at the start: "I have no wish to instruct, and not much to be instructed; my aim is simply to entertain and interest the numerous class of people who, like myself, know nothing of science, but who enjoy speculating and reflecting (not too deeply) upon the phenomena around them. I have therefore allowed myself a loose rein, to run on with whatever came uppermost . . ." (1). But actually Butler came to regard his theory as extremely important, so much so that he wrote to Francis Darwin: "Pitch into it and into me by all means. You cannot do me a greater service than to bundle me neck and crop out of my present position." [17] To his dismay, not one of his opponents seriously tried to do this, even though he wrote four books in his repeated efforts to arouse a response. The Grant Richards, the Huxleys, and the Darwins could not come to grips with Butler on the sophisticated level at which he was prepared to operate.

In *Life and Habit* Butler's intuition moves to the borderline of the known and explores the enigmatic and equivocal operation of the mind. Most readers would grant what he says about the superficial aspects of this subject, but a perceptive reader will follow him into the deeper implications. The better we know something, he argues, the less conscious we are of knowing it; and then it follows that only those things which we do without any consciousness at all are completely known. Thus "perfect knowledge and perfect ignorance" become "extremes which meet. . . . so that the mere fact of conscious knowing or willing implies the presence of more or less novelty and doubt" (15).

In light of these precepts, the kleptomaniac is the only perfect thief, and the greatest hypocrite is the man who "has left off knowing that he is a hypocrite" (18). The man who says: "My belief is that a widely extended good practice must be founded upon Christian doctrine" is less sure of himself than one who says "The Church of England . . . is in fact a church *sui generis*, yielding in point of dignity, purity, and decency of its doctrines, establishment, and ceremonies, to no congregation of Christians in the world" (20-21). This latter statement, Butler says, "is the language of faith, compelled by the exigencies of the occasion to be for a short time conscious of its own existence, but surely very little likely to become so to the extent of feeling the need of any assistance from reason" (21). The same argument holds for infidelity: "It is the unconscious unbeliever who is the true infidel" (21). As an example, he cites the man who asked the Almighty to "change our rulers *as soon as possible*" (22).

IV *Conscious versus Unconscious Knowledge*

Butler explores in this part of his book the revelations of unconscious humor, quoting, for example, Bacon's remark that " 'Reading good books on morality is a little flat and dead.' " He points out that this "is pregnant with painful inferences concerning Bacon's moral character," since it shows that he must have been "reading good books of morality," and yet did not "feel the loathing for further discourses upon the matter which honest people commonly feel now" (23, 24). Thus also when we hear one person praise another for earnestness we feel "that the praiser's attention must have been arrested by sincerity, as by something more or less unfamiliar to himself" (24). He concludes:

"It is only those who are ignorant and uncultivated who can know anything at all in a proper sense of the words. . . . Knowledge is in an inchoate state as long as it is capable of logical treatment" (24-25). Thomas Hardy, in contrasting the suffering of Clem Yoebright, the sophisticated intellectual, to the instinctive happiness of the peasants on Egdon Heath, was exploring the same paradox; but the conclusions Hardy drew were pessimistic, while Butler rejoices in men of intuitive good sense —his Ydgrunites and his Towneleys (Towneley is the suave man-of-the-world whom Ernest admired in *The Way of All Flesh*).

The paradox of the relation between conscious and unconscious knowledge is again well expressed in the following example: "Dog-fanciers tell us that performing dogs never carry their tails; such dogs have eaten of the tree of knowledge, and are convinced of sin accordingly—they know that they know things, in respect of which, therefore, they are no longer under grace, but under the law, and they have yet so much grace left as to be ashamed. So with the human clever dog; he may speak with the tongues of men and angels, but so long as he knows that he knows, his tail will droop" (31). Should we suggest to the Venus de Milo that she learn to read? "Beauty is but knowledge perfected and incarnate. . . . It is not knowledge, then, that is incompatible with beauty; there cannot be too much knowledge, but it must have passed through many people who it is to be feared must be both ugly and disagreeable, before beauty or grace will have anything to say to it" (32).

V Knowledge versus Grace

Butler rejects the idea that science is the coming religion; it is, he says, merely a new superstition which may subject mankind to a more ruthless tyranny than the Church ever did. The so-called scientist "is but medicine-man, augur, priest, in its latest development; useful it may be, but requiring to be well watched by those who value freedom" (35). On the other hand, he writes of the Church: "Do what we may, we are still drawn to the unspoken teaching of her less introspective ages with a force which no falsehood could command. Her buildings, her music, her architecture, touch us as none other on the whole can do; when she speaks there are many of us who think that she denies the deeper truths of her own profounder mind, and unfortunately her tendency is now towards more rather than less introspection. The more she gives way to this—the more she becomes conscious of knowing—the less she will know. But still her ideal is in grace" (34).

The next step in his argument is to include *willing* in the same category as *knowing*. Here he makes an obvious parallel when he says: "we do not will anything utterly and without . . . hesitation, till we have lost sight of the fact that we are exercising our will" (36). Butler finds two classes of actions: those like eating, which must be learned, though they are learned easily, signifying a great readiness to learn them since so many of our ancestors have learned them; and those like swallowing, which we can do at birth because the knowledge is deeper in us and goes back through more generations than the knowledge of eating. We have invented the word "heredity" to explain the ability of the newborn baby to swallow, to digest, to oxidize the blood without previous practice; but the word merely names a difficulty and does not explain it. "Why," Butler asks, "should heredity enable a creature to dispense with the experience which we see to be necessary in all other cases before difficult operations can be performed successfully?" (41). The answer, he suggests, lies in supposing "the continuity of life and sameness between living beings, whether plants or animals, and their descendants, to be far closer than we have hitherto believed" (41). The fact that "we are *most conscious of, and have most control over,* such habits as speech, the upright position, the arts and sciences . . . which are acquisitions peculiar to the human race," and "are *most unconscious of, and have least control over,* our digestion, which we have in common even with our invertebrate ancestry" (42) goes far to prove this. Someday, after many more ages have passed, we will read and write as instinctively as we now circulate our blood. But if human records should be lost, it will take another Harvey to discover that we do so.

VI *Unconscious Knowledge*

Pressing his case further, Butler argues that unborn beings show an uncanny knowledge of what they want and of the means for getting it: The unborn chick grows a tip on its bill with which to peck a hole in its shell exactly as though it knew that such was necessary for it to be born. This unconscious knowledge is perfect because it is the result of infinite practice on the part of the chicken's ancestors; or, we might say, the skill it exhibits shows that *"it is the same chicken which makes itself over and over again"* (61). Butler continues: "What is the discovery of the laws of gravitation as compared with the knowledge which sleeps in every hen's egg upon a kitchen shelf?" (62). "We have established," he concludes, ". . . that all living creatures which show any signs of intelligence, must certainly each one have already gone through the embryonic stages an infinite number of times, or they could no more have achieved the intricate process of self-development unconsciously, than they could play the piano unconsciously without any previous knowledge of the instrument" (63). There is, then, no single stopping point in considering what constitutes personal identity. Each individual is, in a sense, identical with the primordial cell from which he sprang.

Butler also scrutinizes personal identity from the point of view of a given moment, and he discovers that here too the boundaries are far from sharp. We are not only ourselves, but also the sum total of all the influences upon us. "Who shall draw the line," he asks, "between the parasites which are part of us, and the parasites which are not part of us?" (87). Are we not as much "processes of [our] wives or nearest relations" (85-86) as of the corpuscles of our blood? "There is no line possible. Everything melts away into everything else" (87). He proceeds to deduce: "It would appear, then, as though 'we,' 'our souls,' or 'selves,' or 'personalities' . . . are but the *consensus* and full flowing stream of countless sensations and impulses on the part of our tributary souls or 'selves'" (89). And, he asks: "Is it possible to avoid imagining that we may be ourselves atoms, undesignedly combining to form some vaster being, though we are utterly incapable of perceiving that any such being exists?" (90).

VII   *Variations on a Theme*

The possibilities of the lines of thought opened up in *Life and Habit* are amazing, and Butler pursues them one after another like an accomplished composer creating variations on a theme. He considers, for example, that a hen is an egg's way of making another egg: "We see an egg, A, which evidently knows its own meaning perfectly well, and we know that a twelvemonth ago there were two other such eggs, B and C, which have now disappeared, but from which we know A to have been so continuously developed as to be part of the present form of their identity. . . . It would seem, then, unreasonable to deny that A is only B and C come back, with such modifications as they may have incurred since their disappearance" (110).

Similarly, Butler considers what happens to an individual put into surroundings for which its memories have not prepared it, as, for example, a grain of corn put into a hen's stomach. The shock is so great that the grain forgets its own memories and adopts those of the hen, and "there is no such persecutor of grain, as another grain when it has fairly identified itself with a hen" (112). Thus Butler says: "The great question between vast masses of living organism is simply this: 'Am I to put you into a position with which your forefathers have been unfamiliar, or are you to put me into one about which my own have been in like manner ignorant?' Man is only the dominant animal on the earth, because he can, as a general rule, settle this question in his own favour" (113-14).

Again, Butler analyzes the odd ways in which memory operates, showing how long-forgotten chains of recollection can be activated by a chance occurrence, and how often the things we remember best, such as which leg to put first into our trousers on arising, are those we are so unconscious of as not to know that we know them. In like fashion, the caterpillar remembers exactly what to do in each stage of its varied existence. Finally, the infertility of hybrids is obviously explainable by the incompatibility of the divergent memories supplied to the embryo by the parents. Butler quotes from Darwin a description of the failure of five hundred crossbred eggs to mature, and he comments: "No wonder the poor creatures died, distracted as they were by the internal tumult of conflicting memories. . . . Five hundred creatures puzzled to death is not a pleasant subject for contemplation" (142). The memory theory also explains reversions to earlier forms when animals are returned to primitive circumstances: "the creature, in fact, having got into its old groove, remembers it, and takes to all its old ways" (157-58).

VIII *Neuter Insects*

Darwin had cited the example of neuter insects as evidence that the "well-known doctrine of inherited habit as advanced by Lamarck" [18] was untenable. Butler seizes on this and explains at length how his memory theory can account even for the activities of neuter insects. A passage based on an extended analogy exemplifies the literary vividness and humor of his reasoning and shows why he is so exasperating to the scientific brotherhood, unused as it always has been to figurative language:

Or take, again, the constitution of the Church of England. The bishops are the spiritual queens, the clergy are the neuter workers. They differ widely in structure (for dress must be considered as a part of structure), in the delicacy of the food they eat and the kind of house they inhabit, and also in many of their instincts, from the bishops, who are their spiritual parents. Not only this, but there are two distinct kinds of neuter workers—priests and deacons; and of the former there are deans, archdeacons, prebends, canons, rural deans, vicars, rectors, curates, yet all spiritually sterile. In spite of this sterility, however, is there anyone who will maintain that the widely differing structures and instincts of these castes are not due to inherited spiritual habits? Still less will he be inclined to do so when he reflects that by such slight modification of treatment as consecration and endowment any one of them can be rendered spiritually fertile. (194-95)

IX *Attack on Natural Selection*

The reader should not be misled by the humor of passages like these. Butler was very serious indeed in his criticism of the theory of natural selection for he pointed out that it amounts "to little more than to a statement of the fact that when variations have arisen they will accumulate" (203). He felt that we must get "behind the back of 'natural selection,' which is rather a shield and hindrance to our perception of our own ignorance than an explanation of what these causes are" (203). Throughout *Life and Habit* he is indeed trying to get "behind the back of" conventional modes of thinking, and his vivid exposition of the ways of doing so has remarkable power to guide the sympathetic reader. *Life and Habit* is one of the most provocative books to come out of Victorian England.

While working out the theory of his book, Butler had not been

fully aware how closely his views followed in the path of Lamarck, although, of course, by equating heredity with memory
he departed from anything Lamarck had suggested. But his
studies for the work, and especially his rereading of Darwin,
had brought the earlier evolutionary theories to his attention. He
found traces of Lamarckian thought even in Darwin, who continued to maintain that "use and disuse" played a part in natural
selection. To Butler, Lamarck "did not sufficiently link on the experience of the race to that of the individual, nor perceive the
importance of the principle that consciousness, memory, voli-
tion, intelligence, etc., vanish, or become latent, on becoming
intense" (209); but then Butler believed that Lamarck's theories
are "far from having had their last say" (209).

Butler successfully demonstrates that many passages in Darwin
tacitly assume that more than "spontaneous variability" operates
in the origin of species. "To me it seems," Butler wrote, "that the
'Origin of Variation,' whatever it is, is the only true 'Origin of
Species,' and that this must, as Lamarck insisted, be looked for in
the needs and experiences of the creatures varying" (215).
Therefore, he concludes: "The results of competition [referring
to the "survival-of-the-fittest" idea which Darwin had con-
tributed] would be, as it were, the decisions of an arbiter settling
the question whether such and such variation was really to the
animal's advantage or not—a matter on which the animal will,
on the whole, have formed a pretty fair judgment for itself"
(216). He adds: "An animal which discovers the good way will
gradually develop further powers, and so species will get further
and further apart; but the origin of this is to be looked for, not
in the power which decides whether this or that way was good,
but in the cause which determines the creature, consciously or
unconsciously, to try this or that way" (217).

Butler was really fighting for the view that the world contained more than blind chance. He was maintaining that natural
selection is not an adequate explanation or guiding principle and
that biology must have a vitalistic theory if it is to have any theory
at all. To dramatize his point, he cites the leaf moth, which can
imitate leaves in all states of disease and decay. He writes: "I
can no more believe that these artificial fungi in which the moth
arrays itself are due to the accumulation of minute, perfectly
blind, and unintelligent variations, than I can believe that the

artificial flowers which a woman wears in her hat can have got
there without design; or that a detective puts on plain clothes
without the slightest intention of making his victim think that he
is not a policeman" (221). Later he adds, ". . . than I can believe that a mousetrap or a steam-engine is the result of the accumulation of blind fortuitous variations in a creature called
man, which creature has never wanted either mousetraps or
steam-engines, but has had a sort of promiscuous tendency to
make them" (222).

X A Work of Art

Butler concludes his volume *Life and Habit,* as he had other
pieces before, by calling it tentative, a sketch or design for further endeavor "in which I hope to derive assistance from the criticisms which this present volume may elicit" (240). He likens it
to a work of art, the spirit of which is more important than detailed accuracy. But, he adds: "I am in very serious earnest, perhaps too much so, from the first page of my book to the last"
(249). He tells us:

I saw, as it were, a pebble upon the ground, with a sheen that pleased
me; taking it up, I turned it over and over for my amusement, and
found it always grow brighter and brighter the more I examined it. At
length I became fascinated, and gave loose rein to self-illusion. The
aspect of the world seemed changed; the trifle which I had picked up
idly had proved to be a talisman of inestimable value, and had opened
a door through which I caught glimpses of a strange and interesting
transformation. . . . Will the reader bid me wake with him to a
world of chance and blindness? Or can I persuade him to dream with
me of a more living faith than either he or I had as yet conceived as
possible? As I have said, reason points remorselessly to an awakening,
but faith and hope still beckon to the dream." (249-50)

XI *Reception of* Life and Habit

From reviewers or from the professional world Butler received
little assistance in appraising his theory. *The Athenaeum,*[19] although admitting that the book contained "serious and important
scientific truth," suspected a hoax and took Butler to task for his
untenable view of reason. The *Contemporary Review*[20] said: "The
work contains much shrewd sense in a whimsical form"; but it
criticized Butler, on his own principles, for emphasizing his ear-

nestness, and it objected to his attacks on Darwin. The *Westminster Review*[21] advised the general reader and those interested in evolution to read the book which, it avowed, contains "much food for reflection in its pages," and it went on to say that "the incisive touches of the satirist are combined with the more sober suggestions of the scientific critic." Although the *Saturday Review*[22] called the main thesis of *Life and Habit* "a suggestion towards the completion of the Darwinian theory . . . showing the line which future contributions may take," it accused Butler of falling "into the very fallacy of Hartmann," and of being "on the high road to chimaera-land." The *Spectator*[23] likewise attacked Butler's conception of the unconscious, saying that we could never have proof of the existence of the unconscious if it is really unconscious.

Alfred Russel Wallace, co-discoverer with Darwin of the "survival of the fittest" principle, writing in *Nature*,[24] dismissed the book with some faint praise and much condemnation, calling it extreme and perverted; yet he admitted that Butler possessed "'scientific imagination' and logical consistency to a degree very rarely found among scientific men. . . . Though we can at present only consider the work as a most ingenious and paradoxical speculation," Wallace concluded, "it may yet afford a clue to some of the deepest mysteries of the organic world." But in spite of such passages of serious criticism, no one took the trouble to bundle Butler "neck and crop out of [his] present position."

Of course Butler's difficulty was that he had advanced a theory which ran counter to the tendency of science to reduce everything to a single, mechanistic principle. The reasons that his theory could not easily be taken to the laboratory for testing were several. He was appealing to general common sense, to the layman—not to the specialist; he was defending the right of the amateur to have ideas in a scientific field and to be heard; and he was using far-ranging intuitive insight to develop a theory of no immediate practical consequences but one very satisfying to those interested in knowledge for its own sake. We can understand the excitement he felt in evolving his theory linking memory and heredity; he was crossing a really new boundary. We can understand his disappointment, too—even his anger—that the professionals of his age showed no interest in his ideas.

Throughout his life, Butler cherished his intuitive insights and fought for them like a mother for her child. Some of them are so fascinating that it is hard not to admire him for loving them. We may even come to love them ourselves. Butler is like an ancient Greek thinker speculating about atoms, about whether the world is one or many, fire or water. In an age when the inductive method, which he did not revere, reigned supreme, Butler relied on the power of the mind to settle the questions he raised. The world has need of more thinkers—inquisitive, unafraid, willing to defend their conceptions—like Butler. We are perhaps even further today than his contemporaries were from giving such thinkers much opportunity to be heard. It is amazing that *Life and Habit*, as interesting and well argued as it is, should have created so little stir in the world of ideas.

CHAPTER 5

The Battle Joined

I *The History of Evolutionary Thought*

BUTLER'S qualities as a fighter for what he thought true can now be vividly evidenced. To his disappointment over the failure of the theory of *Life and Habit* to win real recognition was soon added the fury of discovering that the party in power in the field of evolutionary speculation did not give credit to earlier investigators and was capable of treating contemporary opponents with contempt. Darwin and Company, he soon convinced himself, were not behaving like honest men; and it was up to him, the Don Quixote of his age, to show their true colors to a world that had been so contentedly hoodwinked. To conclude that Butler tried to kick up this storm because of his own disappointed ambitions is too easy. Rather, the issues themselves should be examined.

While working on *Life and Habit,* Butler had come across indications that the theory of evolution was in a far more advanced stage before the advent of Darwin than was generally admitted. In the third edition of the *Origin of Species* he found "a brief but imperfect sketch" of the history of evolutionary theory which mentioned Buffon, Erasmus Darwin, and Lamarck. When Butler read the works of these men, he was astonished to discover that they had not only often made the same points as Darwin had made, but that their theories were far more satisfactory than Darwin's when they differed from his. In his next book, *Evolution, Old and New* (1879), Butler attempted to establish conclusively the principles of *Life and Habit* by putting them in the perspective of earlier evolutionary speculation. Also, he hoped to bring into question the originality of Darwin.

Butler opened *Evolution, Old and New* by stating as forcefully as he could the reasons for believing in a purposefulness in evolutionary development—a purposefulness in the organism itself, not in a divine creator who stands outside the organic world. The existence of rudimentary organs and of the process of embryonic recapitulation, he argued, supports his view, since it is inconceivable that an all-powerful designer would see fit to retain so much that was apparently useless. He quoted at length from Paley's *Natural Theology*, agreeing enthusiastically with the evidence for design that Paley cited. Butler disagreed, however, that this evidence proved the existence of a forming agent other than the organism itself. "What is commonly conceived of as direct creation by God is moved back to a time and space inconceivable in their remoteness," he wrote, "while the aim and design so obvious in nature are shown to be still at work around us, growing ever busier and busier, and advancing from day to day both in knowledge and power" (35). He then complained that "Mr. Darwin . . . tangled and obscured what his predecessors had made in great part, if not wholly, plain" (36-37).

II *Buffon's Contribution*

In Buffon, Butler discovered a man he could heartily admire. He became convinced that the exigencies of the era had forced Buffon to conceal his real meaning behind protective irony. He complimented Buffon for his skill in doing this: "What he did was to point so irresistibly in the right direction, that a reader of any intelligence should be in no doubt as to the road he ought to take, and then to contradict himself so flatly as to reassure those who would be shocked by a truth for which they were not yet ready" (72).[1] Butler recognized this device in Buffon because on occasion he himself had been forced to use it. Buffon could also write entertaining passages, and "he looked to these parts of his work to keep the whole alive till the time should come when the philosophical side of his writings should be understood and appreciated" (74). Commenting further on Buffon's irony, Butler remarks: "Complaint, then, against an ironical writer on the score that he puzzles us, is a complaint against irony itself; for a writer is not ironical unless he puzzles. He should not puzzle unless he believes that this is the best manner of making his reader understand him in the end . . ." (96).

Evolution, Old and New shows by apt quotation that Buffon did not believe in final causes, for he realized that nature could not tolerate rudimentary organs while working in the light of a clear design. The quotations also show that Buffon recognized inner feelings as a modifying factor and that he was aware of the effect of environment in controlling the spread of living forms. Butler speaks admiringly of Buffon's contempt for science—for its giving of names to things too unimportant to be named and for its assuming that naming is synonymous with explaining. He also discovers to his delight that Buffon had entertained the notion of personal identity through the ages. " 'Man,' " he translates Buffon as saying, " 'and especially educated man, is no longer a single individual. . . . Having discovered the divine art of fixing their thoughts so that they can transmit them to their posterity, [men] become, as it were, one and the same people with their descendants' " (132).

III *The Contribution of Darwin's Grandfather*

In his discussion of Dr. Erasmus Darwin, which follows his study of Buffon, Butler points out that Dr. Darwin believed that individuals are " 'elongations of the parents' " (174); but since he referred instinct to imitation, rather than to memory, he failed to anticipate Butler's own view. Yet Dr. Darwin admitted that "instinct is only reason become habitual" (179). In his discussion of mating, he recognized a "survival-of-the-fittest" factor: " 'The final cause of this contest among the males,' " Dr. Darwin wrote, " 'seems to be *that the strongest and most active animal should propagate the species, which should thence become improved*' " (200). Butler remarks on this: "There have been two factors in modification; the one provides variations, the other accumulates them" (201). Dr. Darwin gives an account of the beaks of different species of birds " 'all [of] which seem to have been gradually produced during many generations *by the perpetual endeavour of the creature to supply the want of food, and to have been delivered to their posterity with constant improvement of them for the purposes required*' " (202).

IV *Lamarck*

Although Butler finds less in Lamarck than in Buffon and Dr. Darwin to please him, he is particularly anxious to rescue Lamarck from neglect because he had been penniless and had had no group around him who could defend his name. There is a psychological factor operating here: Since Butler himself was misunderstood and neglected, he fought with special ardor in behalf of others who, he felt, had suffered a like fate. "Science," Butler remarks with some bitterness, "is not a kingdom into which a poor man can enter easily, if he happens to differ from a philosopher who gives good dinners and has 'his sisters, and his cousins, and his aunts' to play the part of chorus to him" (223). That Lamarck was aware of the part played by environment in evolution is shown by the following quotation: " 'In consequence of the extremely rapid rate of increase of the smaller, and especially of the most imperfect, animals, their numbers would become so great as to prove injurious to the conservation of breeds, and to the progress already made towards more perfect organization, unless nature had taken precautions to keep them down within certain fixed limits which she cannot exceed' " (247). This passage, Butler says, contains all the survival-of-the-fittest "necessary for Lamarck's purpose. . . . Nothing therefore can be more at variance with the truth than to represent Lamarck and the other early evolutionists as ignoring the struggle for existence and the survival of the fittest" (247-48).

The key Lamarckian idea, of course, which has not been demonstrated by more recent research but is necessary to Butler's theory as well as to Darwin's, is the inheritance of acquired characteristics. Lamarck argued that organic development results from sustained use and that the gains thus acquired are transmitted to offspring. Although no evidence to substantiate this view has been forthcoming from the laboratories, it is still possible that something of the sort may be detected; without it, indeed, a coherent theory of evolution is hard to come by. Are we to be reduced to something analogous to the Laputian method of *Gulliver's Travels* of making books? [2] If a monkey pounded on a typewriter for an infinite period of time, all the books in the world would be written by chance. This would be like explaining all the forms of life by chance variation with no inheritance of acquired characteristics. To Butler, this was as good as no explanation at all. "Our modern evolutionists," he says, "should allow that animals are modified not because they subsequently survive, but because they have done this or that which led to their modification, and hence to their surviving" (266).

V *Old Theories Better than New*

After discussing the theories of Patrick Matthew, Etienne and Isidore Geoffroy, and Herbert Spencer, all of whom had preceded Darwin, Butler compares the old and new views. Both views maintain that animals and plants vary, and both hold that variations are transmitted to offspring. But the old view finds the cause of variation in changing conditions of existence, and in "varying needs arising from" (298) these changes, whereas "Mr. Darwin . . . repeatedly avows ignorance, and profound ignorance, concerning the causes of those variations" (299), though he admits the effect of use or disuse, and regards survival of the fittest as "the most important but not the exclusive means of modification" (301). Butler again points out, however, that "natural selection cannot be considered a cause of variation" (304), as Darwin frequently implies that it is; and he says that therefore the *Origin of Species* has no *raison d'être*, that it is "no less a piece of intellectual sleight-of-hand than Paley's *Natural Theology*" (305). The last three chapters of *Evolution, Old and New* are a brilliant display of Butler's power to analyze careless and confusing statements; they go far to confirm his contention that Darwin had no clear conception of his own meaning and that natural selection, as he presents it, is little more than a "will o' the wisp" (327).

VI *Received with Jeers*

The reviewers were outraged by *Evolution, Old and New,* especially by its criticism of Darwin; and, like *Life and Habit,* it was not given a serious examination. It was said to be full of fallacies and verbal quibbles, not to leave "a single clear idea of what it has been driving at." Butler was called crotchety, and he was advised to return to the writing of fiction.[3] Alfred R. Wallace, however, discussed the book more seriously in a leading article in *Nature,*[4] calling it interesting and useful, and stating that Butler's hypothesis, supported by the historical background he provides, forms "an important and even a necessary supplement to the theory advocated by Mr. Darwin." He agreed with Butler's evaluation of Buffon, but he refused in conclusion to find any force in Butler's attack on Darwin.

VII *The* Kosmos *Affair*

In November, 1879, a book entitled *Erasmus Darwin* was published with a preliminary notice by Charles Darwin. In this preface, Darwin said that the body of the book was a translation from the German of an article by Ernest Krause which had appeared in *Kosmos* before *Evolution, Old and New* was written.[5] When Butler read the new work, he was amazed to find Krause stating in his conclusion that "Erasmus Darwin's system was in itself a most significant first step in the path of knowledge which his grandson has opened up for us; but the wish to revive it at the present day, as has actually been seriously attempted, shows a weakness of thought and a mental anachronism which no one can envy." Butler also found quotations from Buffon using the exact wording of his own translations from the French. There were other evidences that the work was a covert attack upon him.

After hastily learning enough German to serve his purpose, Butler compared the translation with the German original and found that much material, including the final six pages, had been added. The work was thus not what Darwin's preface said that it was—a translation of an article written before *Evolution, Old and New*. Butler immediately wrote to Charles Darwin for an explanation. Darwin replied that alterations in translations were "so common a practice that it never occurred to me to state that the article had been modified."[6] This explanation did not satisfy Butler, who, having informed Darwin that he was going to do so, proceeded to air the matter in a letter to *The Athenaeum*.[7] Darwin wished to answer this letter. He wanted to point out that, when he first wrote to Butler, he had forgotten that the printer had inadvertently omitted from the book a statement that the text was a revision. Though his son, Francis Darwin, felt that Darwin should reply, Huxley advised against any rejoinder.[8] "A clever and unscrupulous man like Mr. Butler," Darwin wrote to Huxley, indicating his own fearfulness, "would be sure to twist whatever I may say against me."[9] Some months later, after *Unconscious Memory* had appeared with an account of the whole matter, Francis Darwin again wished his father to make a public statement. This time it was Leslie Stephen who advised against it.

Thus Butler was never to learn that the whole affair had originated in an error compounded by forgetfulness and bad advice. At the very least, his anger was justified, if only by the cowardliness of those who told the aging Darwin to refuse an explanation which could have been so simply provided. In 1904 Francis Darwin wrote his sister that he had omitted the controversy when he edited his father's letters, but added "I now think he [Butler] had some cause of complaint, though he entirely lost his head and behaved abominably." [10]

VIII *Fighting for a Principle*

Butler had assuredly been given provocation for bad behavior. But the steps that he took were taken in behalf of a principle as much as in defense of himself. He had become convinced that "people who are above suspicion," this time the scientists, would stop at nothing to defeat an adversary and to secure their own comfort, and he wished to present an example of how low they would stoop—an example that would be so forceful as to make his point unforgettable. He wanted to "give old Darwin the best warming that I can manage to give him—and I think I shall manage a pretty hot one" [11]; this because for him Darwin epitomized the high priest who puts an end to freedom. Unfortunately, he did not realize that many readers would interpret his defense as entirely personal and would come to regard him as paranoiac. [12]

Unconscious Memory begins with an account of what the *Origin of Species* had meant to its first readers who did not probe its exact meaning carefully enough to discover that it did not fully explain what it appeared to explain. After a brief résumé of his own writings on evolution, Butler shows that Darwin carefully covered his tracks and left the impression that no major work had been done with the theory of evolution before his own. Much of the analysis in this part of his book is based on a subtle reading between the lines and upon inferences regarding Darwin's hidden motives. With skillful citation of texts and analysis of grammatical vagueness, Butler cuts through the complexities and makes out a case that is convincing and effective.

The tone becomes progressively more angry and culminates in direct charges of unscrupulous behavior in the account of the *Kosmos* article affair. Butler had wanted a fight "according to the rules of the game," but he was convinced that his opponents were capable of hitting below the belt. There is little doubt that Huxley, the journalist and science reviewer Grant Allen, and Darwin himself failed to understand the issues at stake in the quarrel as clearly as Butler did. Nor did they appreciate the importance of meticulous honesty in dealing with an opponent and in presenting the history of an idea.

Although one critic has speculated that Butler attacked Darwin because Darwin was a father image to him,[13] and although others feel that he was motivated by outraged egotism, the fact of the matter is that he was in a strong position and made the most of it in forensic style. In return, he received the bitterest treatment that can be handed out to a man looking for vigorous debate—silence. Or worse still, in our time, the insolent comments that he was an exhibitionist, a show-off, a neurotic. "Don't bother about me or my bad behavior," he might say to his modern detractors, were he alive today. "Bother about the issues. What do you say to them?"

That Butler never regarded his quarrel with Darwin as a passing affair is shown by his request to Streatfeild shortly before his death that *Unconscious Memory*, the most quarrelsome book he had ever written, should be reissued in a new edition (xiv). "When I thought," he had written in that book,

of Buffon, of Dr. Erasmus Darwin, of Lamarck, and even of the author of the *Vestiges of Creation*, to all of whom Mr. Darwin had dealt the same measure which he was now dealing to myself; when I thought of these great men, now dumb, who had borne the burden and heat of the day, and whose laurels had been filched from them; of the manner, too, in which Mr. Darwin had been abetted by those who should have been the first to detect the fallacy which had misled him; of the hotbed of intrigue which science has now become; of the disrepute into which we English must fall as a nation if such practices as Mr. Darwin had attempted in this case were to be tolerated;—when I thought of all this, I felt that though prayers for the repose of dead men's souls might be unavailing, yet a defence of their work and memory, no matter against what odds, might avail the living, and resolved that I would do my utmost to make my countrymen aware of the spirit now ruling among those whom they delight to honour.

(53-54)

IX *Hering and von Hartmann*

After setting his case before the public, Butler goes on in *Unconscious Memory* to present the theory of a German scientist, Ewald Hering, who in 1870 had read to the Imperial Academy of Sciences at Vienna a statement of his thesis that heredity is linked to memory and that memory can be traced to minute vibrations common to all matter and thus is a universal property. In general, Butler insisted on his right to stand on common sense and not to raise questions that were too remotely speculative; but Hering's suggestions intrigued him because they seemed to provide a basis for his own views and thus he found them a valuable addition to his *Life and Habit* theory. In the section on "Vibrations" in Jones' edition of the *Note-Books*, Butler explores the matter further. Characteristically, he says: "I was alarmed by the suggestion and fathered it upon Professor Hering who never, that I can see, meant to say anything of the kind, but I forced my view on him, as it were, by taking hold of a sentence or two in his lecture . . ." (61).

In *Unconscious Memory* Butler also presents an extract from von Hartmann's *Philosophy of the Unconscious* which he translated for this occasion.[14] He had been accused of falling into "the fallacy of von Hartmann" in his use of unconscious memory in *Life and Habit*; but, on studying the German author, he found the unconscious conceived of as a mysterious, clairvoyant agency so far from the simple idea that he had himself presented that it repelled him. He rejected it emphatically. His notes on various passages in the text are an acute analysis of the basic differences between his view and the German scientist's, and the points he makes reveal also, we imagine, what reservations he might have concerning the Freudian unconscious were he alive today. One telling observation he makes is that instinctive or unconscious knowledge is always the result of long-repeated, conscious effort; it is not something generically different from and below consciousness. At the end of his book he discusses the reasons why a memory theory is called for and why a purely mechanistic view will not suffice to explain the actions of organic beings. He also suggests that there must be incipient traces of mind even in the inorganic world. Without any matter, there would be no mind, he says, and, without any mind, there would be no matter.

X *Attack and Defense*

Butler hoped that his direct attack on Darwin would get him a hearing, but he was disappointed. Very few reviewers paid any attention to *Unconscious Memory*. The *Athenaeum*[15] complained of "the gradual decline in the literary qualities" of Butler's work.

George J. Romanes, in a front-page article in *Nature*,[16] attacked
Butler savagely, calling his book a "sorry exhibition" and Butler
"an upstart ignoramus." Romanes continues: "A man who in the
full light of Darwin's theory can deliberately return to the weak
and beggarly elements of Lamarck—such a man shows only that
in judgment he is still a child." Butler had to threaten legal action
to force *Nature* to print a letter from him in which he reiterated
that no one had yet answered his charges that Darwin had dealt
in misrepresentation.[17] Romanes replied with further abuse.

It is interesting to note, however, that Butler did eventually
win support. In 1884, when *The Athenaeum* reviewed Romanes
own work, *Mental Evolution in Animals,* it took Romanes severely
to task for not even mentioning that Butler had originated a
theory which Romanes now called his own.[18] "We have previously
called attention to Mr. Butler's views as deserving a hearing by
professional biologists. . . . This attention has now been paid to
Mr. Butler's work, but it must be regretted that more attention
has not been paid to Mr. Butler's feelings and to Mr. Butler's
rights over the valuable suggestions he has made to students of
descent which, it would seem from the book before us, are henceforth to be adopted as an integral part of Darwinistic doctrine."
When Romanes replied defending himself,[19] the reviewer pointed
out that between 1859 and 1883 in which latter year "Mr. Romanes devotes more than half of his treatment of instinct to inherited memory," Mr. Butler had produced *Life and Habit.*
"We therefore venture to attribute the advance in Mr. Romanes'
views about instinct to the influence of Mr. Butler's work. . . .
We still remain unconvinced by Mr. Romanes' argument that he
has satisfied the laws of literary courtesy." The controversy continued with two more letters from Romanes, two from the reviewer, and one each from Professor Ray Lankester, Herbert
Spencer, and Butler himself. But nothing really important ever
came of this exchange.

CHAPTER 6

Undefeated

I *The Dedicated Author*

IN his discussion of Erasmus Darwin in *Evolution, Old and New,* Butler had said: "If his opponents, not venturing to dispute with him, passed over one book in silence, he should have followed it up with another, and another, and another, year by year, as Buffon and Lamarck did; it is only thus that men can expect to succeed against vested interests" (173). This was exactly what Butler was doing, although hard-pressed financially and disappointed with each of his books that, in turn, did not pay its own way. He kept hoping for a change in his fortunes, however, and was fairly certain of eventual success (*Note-Books,* 6). It was not to come in his lifetime, but he was quite right about his ability to succeed. If Butler could have received just a few cents royalty on each copy of *The Way of All Flesh,* for example, that has been sold since its publication, how wealthy he would have been! At this time (1884) he wrote: "My books are to me much the most important thing in life. They are, in fact, 'me' much more than anything else." [1]

In March, 1884, Butler published a volume of *Selections from Previous Works, with Remarks on Romanes' "Mental Evolution in Animals" and "A Psalm of Montreal."* Most reviewers ignored this new book, but *The Athenaeum* [2] gave it a very favorable review. "These lively pages," it said, "contain selections from works which are likely to exercise considerable influence on the most prominent doctrine of the age, the theory of evolution. . . . Mr. Butler's service to students of descent consists in the prominent way in which he has called attention to the causes, as distinct from the fact, of evolution. . . . In identifying heredity and memory Mr. Butler is on the highest wave of contemporary speculation." The reviewer also remarked that Butler's literary style was "infinitely superior to that of any other writer on evolution, with the exception of Prof. Huxley."

II *The Attack Renewed*

In spite of the poor sale of the *Selections*—it was the most unsuccessful of all Butler's books—he reentered the evolutionary lists in 1887 with a new volume, *Luck, or Cunning?* In his preface he says that he "became more and more convinced," in the course of his writing, "that no progress could be made towards a sounder view of the theory of descent until people came to understand what the late Mr. Charles Darwin's theory of natural selection amounted to. . . . Until the mindless theory of Charles-Darwinian natural selection was finally discredited, and a mindful theory of evolution was substituted in its place . . . my own theories could [not] stand much chance of being attended to" (xvii). Later he speaks of Darwin's "pitchforking . . . of mind out of the universe," but "so thickly had he gilded" the pill he was giving us "with descent with modification" that we "swallowed it without a murmur. . . . Indeed, we have even given life pensions to some of the most notable of these biologists" who supported Darwin, "I suppose to reward them for having hoodwinked us so much to our satisfaction" (6).

Butler is arguing again as he had always argued. Instead of seeing science as a specialized game played by specialized rules which only operate well when intangibles like intelligence are omitted from the reckoning, instead of conforming to the materialism of the age, he is raising an outcry because, in his view, the game must be played with a wider reference—with an awareness of the meaningfulness of life. The point of view and the attitude one has are all important, and the matter must first of all be fought out on the philosophical level. It is in the final analysis not a game but a matter of life and death.

All the details and examples Butler has amassed are presented in an attempt to win his opponents by speaking in terms they can understand, but the real argument is rationalistic, not empirical. The battle is about what kind of a universe we must have to give a habitation to our aspirations. Butler has put his finger on a major cause of disillusionment in his world and in the twentieth century: the conviction that it makes no ultimate difference what anyone does. He is saying that if we think carefully enough, we may discover that things as they exist do not have to be so. The scientists are not necessarily right. Let us break free, he urges, from the dictatorship of the men in the laboratory who do not really understand the ultimate meaning of their work. Later editions of Darwin's book, Butler tells us, "bore abundant traces of the fray." But will his followers give in?

Butler defends the right of a literary man to interest himself in a scientitific subject. He defends the right of such a man to use facts he himself has not collected, just as an architect builds with stones he did not quarry. Yet he admits that his speculations have caused him much anxiety:

I must confess that I have found it [my theory] somewhat of a white elephant. It has got me into the hottest of hot water, made a literary Ishmael of me, lost me friends whom I have been sorry to lose, cost me a good deal of money, done everything to me, in fact, which a good theory ought not to do. Still, as it seems to have taken up with me, and no one else is inclined to treat it fairly, I shall continue to report its developments from time to time as long as life and health are spared me. Moreover, Ishmaels are not without their uses, and they are not a drug in the market just now.   (14)

In his own way, Butler enjoyed his fight and his anomalous position.

III   *The Psychology of Changing Ideas*

In *Luck, or Cunning?* Butler states again that opinions—even scientific opinions—are a function of what people are used to believing. The view that each individual is just himself and has no physical or psychical connections with his ancestors works nine times out of ten, he says, comparing it with his own theory of identity of the generations:

Neither view is more true than the other, but the one was wanted every hour and minute of the day, and was therefore kept, so to speak, in stock, and in one of the most accessible places of our mental store-house, while the other was so seldom asked for that it became not worth while to keep it. By-and-by it was found so troublesome to send out for it, and so hard to come by even then, that people left off selling it at all, and if any one wanted it he must think it out at home as best he could; this was troublesome, so by common consent the world

decided no longer to busy itself with the continued personality of successive generations—which was all very well until it also decided to
busy itself with the theory of descent with modification. On the introduction of a foe so inimical to many of our pre-existing ideas the balance of power among them was upset, and a readjustment became
necessary, which is still far from having attained the next settlement
that seems likely to be reasonably permanent. (18-19)

Continuing along this line, he remarks: "Ideas can be changed
to almost any extent in almost any direction, if the change is
brought about gradually and in accordance with the rules of all
development. As in music we may take almost any possible dis-
cord with pleasing effect if we have prepared and resolved it
rightly, so our ideas will outlive and outgrow almost any modification which is approached and quitted in such a way as to fuse the
old and new harmoniously" (20). To avoid stagnation we must
have changes in the mental as well as in the physical spheres, he
argues; but the changes must be by infinitesimals if they are to
survive. Obviously, he is again giving himself a lesson about the
danger of pushing too fast and too far, in addition to making a
good general point. "If we have faith," he says, "we can so work
these miracles [of change] as Orpheus-like to charm denizens of
the unseen world into the seen again—provided we do not look
back, and provided also we do not try to charm half a dozen
Eurydices at a time" (23).

Butler rejects the claim made by Herbert Spencer that the
theory linking heredity and memory was implicit in his own work
by examining all the relevant passages and by showing that it
was not. In the course of his discussion he comments on the fact
that "contradictions in terms" while sometimes "very dreadful
things," are nevertheless the basis of intellectual consciousness;
they are "the very small deadlocks without which there is no
going . . . on a small scale [they] please or pain as the case may
be; on a larger, give an ecstasy of pleasure, or shock to the extreme of endurance; and on a still larger, kill whether they be on
the right side or the wrong" (33).

He then examines Romanes' *Mental Evolution in Animals*
closely, showing how often it makes use of the *Life and Habit*
theory, though adding that "at the same time that I claim the
weight of Mr. Romanes' authority, I am bound to admit that I do
not find his support satisfactory" (40). Romanes claimed that

heredity plays an important part in forming memory, Butler says; but though he treated heredity as an active agent, yet nowhere did he explain what it was. Butler in this discussion again tracks down and exposes the inconsistencies and inaccuracies in much of the technical writing of his time.

IV *Stylistic Analysis*

Since Butler himself had the courage of his convictions and was willing to call a spade a spade, it was easy for him to spot passages in other writers which beat around the bush or which had confused meanings. Anyone interested in good science writing should carefully study Butler's analysis of this kind of subterfuge. For example, we take the following: Romanes had written, "Profound, however, as our ignorance unquestionably is concerning the physical substratum of memory, I think we are at least justified in regarding this substratum as the same both in ganglionic or organic, and in the conscious or psychological memory, seeing that the analogies between them are so numerous and precise" (42). Butler translates this as "the analogies between the memory with which we are familiar in daily life, and heredity memory [are] 'so numerous and precise' as to justify us in considering them as of one and the same kind" (42). He goes on to show that Romanes reverses himself as his discussion proceeds, and he also points out that his language is confused because he does not want us to discover that he is hunting with the hounds and running with the hare.

Darwin, Butler reminds us, often did the same thing. "It will take years to get the evolution theory out of the mess in which [he] has left it. He was heir to a discredited truth; he left behind him an accredited fallacy. Mr. Romanes, if he is not stopped in time, will get the theory connecting heredity and memory into just such another muddle as Mr. Darwin has got evolution, for surely the writer who can talk about *heredity being able to work up* the faculty of homing into the instinct of migration' . . . is little likely to depart from the usual methods of scientific procedure with advantage either to himself or any one else" (45).

Butler obviously had a great deal of fun writing *Luck, or Cunning?*. He traced down the shifting statements on instinct in the various editions of the *Origin of Species*, demonstrating that Darwin reversed himself again and again. He accused Darwin of never saying anything unequivocally because he always wanted to hedge. He finds the *Times* reporting that the theory of natural selection is not really a theory of the origin of species, and then complimenting Romanes for making "the most important addition to the theory of evolution since . . . the *Origin of Species*." "Considering," says Butler, "that the *Times* has just implied the main thesis of the *Origin of Species* to be one which does not stand examination, this is rather a doubtful compliment" (50).

V *The Argument for Design*

In a chapter on "The Question at Issue," Butler states the argument for design as clearly as he can, but he brings out many metaphorical implications. He says, however, that he is merely developing the views expressed by Lamarck and Erasmus Darwin. The struggle between change—life—and the *status quo*—death—, he tells us, is universal; and one or other have "to re-enter into the womb from whence they came and be born again in some form which shall give greater satisfaction" (56). It is surprising that our author did not see that some of his passages are a kind of scientific poetry and that it would be a long time before the prosaic mind of materialistic cause-and-effect philosophers could grasp them. Perhaps he did see this, yet the hope of acceptance bloomed perennial in his heart. In all honesty, what could he expect Grant Allen, Huxley, and Romanes to make of him? He was surely, as he says in his first chapter, writing for later generations.

From the successive editions of the *Origin of Species*, Butler also presents telling examples of the "numerous, successive, slight alterations" Darwin made. Butler comments that in them "the working of Mr. Darwin's mind can be seen as though it were the twitchings of a dog's nose" (76), and he adds that from them an "idea can be formed of the difficulty in which he found himself involved by his initial blunder of thinking he had got a distinctive feature which entitled him to claim the theory of evolution as an original idea of his own" (76). Butler then repeats the point he made in *Evolution, Old and New*, that Buffon, Dr. Darwin, and Lamarck all recognized the presence of chance in evolution. But he contends that they, unlike Charles Darwin, realized that chance alone could not explain the facts. Darwin, he says, places all the emphasis on luck, whereas a sound view recognizes that cunning is more important and indeed absolutely necessary. "Can there be a moment's hesitation," he asks, "in admitting that if capital is found to have been developed largely, continuously, by many people, in many ways, over a long period of time, it can only have been by means of continued application, energy, effort, industry, and good sense? Granted there has been luck too; of course there has, but let it go without saying. . . . A foolish organism and its fortuitous variation will be soon parted, for, as a general rule, unless the variation has so much connection with the organism's past habits and ways of thought as to be in no proper sense of the word 'fortuitous,' the organism will not know what to do with it when it has got it" (95-96).

Later in *Luck, or Cunning?* Butler returns to his Erewhonian argument that machines have a kind of life. Using the new conception of protoplasm as the basic living unit, he points out that many parts of the body, such as bones and nails, contain no protoplasm. Are we to call them dead? If not, then hammers and saws and hats and shoes which we habitually use are living too, though on a slightly more remote level than bones and nails. If so, then protoplasm may also be dead, since it contains substances like oxygen and hydrogen which are not protoplasm, and animals are machines. Indeed, he points out, the neo-Darwinian evolution (Charles Darwin's), by enthroning chance also enthrones mechanism; for there remains no legitimate function for thought and feeling: everything would go on just as it does if neither of these existed.

Butler is as certain as the Duke of Argyll,[3] whom he quotes, that Darwin's followers have attempted to read mind out of the universe; but it is worth noting his disagreement with the Duke's remark that "a reign of terror" has been established. "It is hardly possible," Butler comments, "for any one to oppose the fallacy involved in the Charles-Darwinian theory of natural selection more persistently and unsparingly than I have done myself from the year 1877 onwards; naturally I have at times been very angrily attacked in consequence, and as a matter of business have made myself as unpleasant as I could in my rejoinders, but I cannot remember anything having been ever attempted against me which could cause fear in any ordinarily constituted person" (124).

VI *Boundaries*

Butler gives careful consideration to the problem of boundaries, pointing out that if we follow one tendency of seeing the similarities in things—life and death, for example, or luck and cunning—we end up with one universal, and all distinctions vanish. But if we follow the tendency of emphasizing differences, we find ourselves with as many names for things as there are atoms. This line of argument reminds us of William James's *A Pluralistic Universe.*[4] Thus, Butler says, "There is never either absolute design rigorously pervading every detail, nor yet absolute absence of design . . . we should admit that both design and chance, however well defined, each have an aroma, as it were, of the other" (131). So out of harmony with the spirit of his age does he feel, he tells us, that he sometimes wonders whether he is the victim of hallucination—had some malicious fiend given him a different Darwin to look at from the Darwin everyone else saw? "Nevertheless I know," he says, "that either every canon, whether of criticism or honourable conduct, which I have learned to respect is an impudent swindle, . . . or else that Mr. Darwin and his supporters are misleading the public" (141).

After a lengthy presentation of further evidence that Darwin continually claimed the doctrine of survival of the fittest as his own and carefully avoided giving any credit to his predecessors, Butler examines Grant Allen's biography of Darwin. The fun he has with a passage from Allen is another good example of his method of attack. Allen had written of Darwin's view of the increments in brain power in contrast to Spencer's Lamarckian view: "I venture to think that the first way, if we look it clearly in the face, will seem to be practically unthinkable. . . ." Butler remarks:

I like our looking a 'way' which is 'practically unthinkable' 'clearly in the face.' I particularly like 'practically unthinkable.' I suppose we can think it in theory, but not in practice. I like almost everything Mr. Allen says or does; it is not necessary to go far in search of his good things; dredge up any bit of mud from him at random and we are pretty sure to find an oyster with a pearl in it, if we look it clearly in the face; I mean, there is sure to be something which will be at any rate 'almost' practically unthinkable.   (189-190)

Luck, or Cunning? concludes with a discussion of Ray Lankester's attack on Lamarck and with a chapter "Per Contra" on Darwin's merits, wherein we are told that "Mr. Darwin played for his own generation, and he got in the very amplest measure the recognition which he endeavoured, as we all do, to obtain" (215).

VII *Hisses Again*

If Butler hoped to make headway by writing "book after book" on evolution, he was disappointed. *The Athenaeum*[5] said it regretted "to see a mind of considerable power frittered away in ephemeral conflict," adding: "We have from the first acknowledged Mr. Butler's merits as an acute thinker on the problems of evolution." Some months later, when Butler wrote to *The Athenaeum* about another matter, he commented on the untruth of this statement: *Life and Habit* and *Unconscious Memory* had both been condemned in *The Athenaeum*.[6] *The Academy*[7] published a review by Grant Allen which considered none of the points Butler made but praised him in equivocal terms:

The hardest heart could not fail to be touched by the profound pathos of Mr. Samuel Butler's Op. 8. . . . In the first place, here is a work of consummate ingenuity, rare literary skill, and a certain happy vein of sardonic humor—a work pregnant with epigram, sparkling with wit, and instinct throughout with a powerful original fancy—flung out upon the world in the uncongenial guise of a scientific treatise. . . . He stands by himself, a paradoxer of the first water, hopeless and friendless, at least in the desert of the present generation. . . . He is made of the very stuff that heroes and martyrs and madmen are made of. . . . Filled with righteous wrath against the Frankenstein of his own brain [his view of Darwin], he goes forth now, a biological Quixote, to wage a holy war against the wicked giant he has laboriously invented for his personal vexation. . . . I have seldom read a more delightful and readable book, in its own way, than *Luck or Cunning*. It is a most valuable, original, and suggestive contribution to current evolutionary thought. The author of *Erewhon* has at bottom something to say.

CHAPTER 7

Pastures New

I *A Busy Life*

BUTLER'S books on evolution represent him at the height of his power. They constitute a very important part of his life's work and contain many passages as lively, as original, and as provocative as anything he wrote. No serious student of his work can ignore them. Like his other books, they demand a good deal of the reader and will carry him across some boundaries if he dares to let them, but, as we have seen, not without a certain danger to his settled views of life. Yet, in spite of the effort these books cost Butler, during the decade from 1876 to 1886 he was also engaged in completing *The Way of All Flesh,* and in many other activities. Although he had given up the idea of painting as a profession, he continued his art work, and kept submitting pictures to the Royal Academy. After 1876 they were always rejected.[1] "Mr. Heatherley's Holiday," exhibited in 1874, shows Mr. Heatherley working on a skeleton with classical casts in the background. It can be viewed as a symbolic representation of Butler's own life-to-come during the following years, as can the picture of Don Quixote exhibited in 1876 and the rejected picture of a knight in armor submitted with three others, also refused. In 1886, in his most serious attempt to enter the world of institutionalism of which he was so critical, he applied for the Slade Professorship of Art at Cambridge but was unsuccessful.

In 1876 Butler had made the acquaintance of Henry Festing Jones, who was to become his devoted friend and eventually his biographer. Among other occupations Jones was a student of music and had been doing some composing. In 1883, after Butler had urged him to write in the manner of Handel, saying he was sure it could be done, Jones said to him: "Very well, then, do it and show it to me." When they met some days later at Heatherley's, Butler played a minuet he had composed to meet the chal-

lenge.[2] For the next two years the two worked together and in
1885 they published their *Gavottes, Minuets, Fugues, and Other
Short Pieces for the Piano.* They took lessons in harmony and
continued their collaboration in the composition of *Narcissus: a
Cantata in the Handelian Form,* published in 1888. Some of
Butler's contributions to these two works are delightful. Although
written in the manner of Handel, they are more than merely imi-
tative. In 1890 Butler wrote his sister May about the pleasure he
felt on hearing of a girl who played his music to her friends and
called it *"des oeuvres posthumes de Handel."* [3] After Butler's
death, Jones completed his part of the work on *Ulysses: an Oratorio* and published it in 1904. Butler's whole life was so steeped
in Handel that one key to the understanding of his work can be
found in the vigorous rhythms, melodic sweetness, and self-
confident mastery of that great artist. Butler once remarked
that not a day of his life had passed without a passage from Handel going through his mind. One of his last requests as he lay dying was for the score of *Solomon.*

II   *The Heavenly Kingdom*

Even when hard pressed for money, Butler had insisted upon
an annual vacation. He attributed his ability to keep going—
despite multiform discouragements and the tension caused by his
thinking beyond the confines of his era—to the fact that he made
these breaks and fortified himself with impressions from another,
healthier world.[4] One result of his travels was that in 1880 his
publisher offered him £100 for an illustrated book about Italy,[5] if
he would write one; and by mid-1881 Miss Savage was reading
the completed manuscript with delight.[6] When the publisher did
not like the work and rejected it, Butler published it in the fall at
his own expense. This book, *Alps and Sanctuaries*—his most re-
laxed, casual work—is a tribute to Butler's heavenly kingdom,
Italy, and a record of the thoughts which passed through his
mind while he was in the land where so many of the theories of
Life and Habit applied, where the inhabitants seemed to him to
have achieved so much unconscious perfection. In many respects
this work is the antipiece to *The Way of All Flesh,* that excoriating exposé of the evils wrought by self-conscious righteousness.
Alps and Sanctuaries is also profusely illustrated with drawings
Butler made of the places he wrote about, and it contains many

passages from Handel which accompanied Butler just as they did the hero of *Erewhon*. The student of Butler will find this travel book rewarding reading, but the general reader may find it too digressive.

Since both Handel and Shakespeare made use of Italian material, Butler opens his volume with a comparison of them. He places Handel as much above Shakespeare for his unconscious power as Shakespeare is above other men. In discussing the St. Gotthard pass, entryway to Italy, Butler discourses on the importance of knowing what we really like and of not being led by fashion. We remember that in *The Way of All Flesh* he makes fun of George Pontifex for his conventional raptures on viewing this pass (Chapter 4). He has great faith in the creative ability of the mind that knows itself. How like William James's "Will to Believe" is the following: ". . . 'the longing after immortality,' though not indeed much of an argument in favour of our being immortal at the present moment, is perfectly sound as a reason for concluding that we shall one day develop immortality, if our desire is deep enough and lasting enough" (7).

III   *Renewed Faith*

During the years, Butler's thoughts about religion had mellowed from his New Zealand days when he had said he was renouncing Christianity altogether. He was now too aware of the problematic nature of human reason to wish any longer to be so sure of himself. He held views which, he felt, were not far from those held by his father and by every right-thinking man of the Church of England. As he had written in *Life and Habit*, the unintrospective beliefs of the Church, hallowed by long tradition, had more of truth in them than the new discoveries of the scientific pioneers. *Alps and Sanctuaries* conveys successfully much of the spirit of the Italian faith and is so full of respect for this traditional wisdom that it pleased many Catholic readers. Butler recalls an anecdote of an Italian woman in London who, missing the wayside shrines, said her prayers before a dentist's showcase; and he asks: "Which of us, indeed, does not sit contentedly enough upon chalk eggs at times?" (26). He then ascribes to the power of illusion much of the progress of mankind, and suggests that "the human intellect owes its superiority over that of the lower animals in great measure to the stimulus which alcohol has given to imagination" (27). In other words, worthy results can arise from unworthy causes. Thus with religion: The effect of their faith on the people of Italy argues that it must somehow be right after all, even if the probing intellect rejects it.

IV *Change and Paradox*

Butler speculates on the marvelous effect of crossing: of stimulating one way of being or line of thought by infusion from something different, but something not too different. He comments, too, on the growth in geometrical ratio of inventions, though observing that at each stage the inventors are "repudiated" and come "to a bad end" (42). Developments which previously took a thousand years have occurred in a hundred years; now they take ten years; soon they will take one year, then a tenth of a year, and so on. "It follows by an easy process of reasoning," he observes, "that, after another couple of hundred years or so, great sweeping changes should be made several times in an hour, or indeed in a second, or fraction of a second, till they pass unnoticed as the revolutions we undergo in the embryonic stages, or are felt simply as vibrations" (43). He concludes that the present time (1880) is the only "comfortable time for a man to live in. . . . The past was too slow, and the future will be too fast," thus taking a stand in favor of the very world which was so unreceptive to his own constant needling. From this he goes on to the idea that "science is rapidly reducing time and space to a very undifferentiated condition."

Butler indeed is acquiring a mellower understanding of the value of paradox in life. He purposely misquotes Tennyson: "There lives more doubt in honest faith" (48), and then calmly comments: "It is a bad sign for a man's peace in his own convictions when he cannot stand turning the canvas of his life occasionally upside down, or reversing it in a mirror, as painters do with their pictures" (50). But he builds no argument for revolt on this sad fact. However, he admires the Catholics in Italy especially because they can do this. He refers to the fool's mass of the medieval church and the gargoyles of Gothic cathedrals as evidence of the robustness of faith. "I would persuade all Jews, Mohammedans, Comtists, and freethinkers to turn high Anglicans, or better still, downright Catholics for a week in every year," he writes. "It is a great grief to me that there is no place where I can go among Mr. Darwin, Professors Huxley, Tyndall and Ray Lankester . . . as I can go among the Italian priests" (50-51).

V *An Appealing Picture*

These passages of speculation make up only a part of *Alps and Sanctuaries;* in the rest we get glimpses of Italian peasants and townspeople drawn with love, humor, and affection; of fascinating little villages nestled in the mountains above the Val Leventina; and of the author walking the trails in various seasons and weathers. All of this makes the reader long to visit northern Italy, for he feels that he would love it as Butler did. The health and good spirits of the inhabitants are repeatedly noted, and their unself-conscious faith and absorption in life are contrasted with the puritanical self-consciousness and righteousness of the English.

Catholics, Butler believes, have the logical advantage over Protestants; but "reasonable people will look with distrust upon too much reason" (86). The important things in life—body, soul, money—are all taken on faith; faith and reason must go together, and are fused in what we call temper. "If it is asked, In what should a man have faith? . . . the answer is, [in] the current feeling among those whom he most looks up to—looking upon himself with suspicion if he is either among the foremost or the laggers" (88). This is Butler's conservatism, his Laodiceanism, his *surtout point de zèle.* But remembering his own creative life, we can believe that he did not misapply his doctrine. Indeed, he used only enough of the mood of *Alps and Sanctuaries* to keep himself alive.

Among the most charming episodes of the book are the accounts Butler gives of his sojourns in out-of-the-way inns usually frequented only by Italians. Here his sensitivity comes into play, his ability to love and appreciate these people for their naturalness and their breeding which, he says, is as much above that of the English as the English are above the colonists. His account of Cricco, the servant, is delightful, as is also that of the picnic with Professor Vela when Butler was left with the impression that he "was among the nicest and most lovable people in the world" (222). *Alps and Sanctuaries* certainly should be better known than it is. Who, after reading it, could accuse Butler of coldness and heartlessness?

VI *No Art for Art's Sake*

A chapter on the decline of Italian art presents our author's view of the sources of artistic effectiveness. Priggishness, he says, is the besetting sin of Englishmen, which will last as long as Oxford and Cambridge universities last. Art in Italy has declined for priggish reasons—its contemporary painters are interested, not in painting out of love for a particular subject but in the desire to paint an academic picture. "The date of the opening of the Bolognese Academy coincides . . . with the complete decadence of Italian art" (126), he asserts. The trouble with the academic system is that it trains artists to study other men's work rather than nature. "As for the old masters," he adds, "the better plan would be never even to look at one of them, and to consign Raffaelle, along with Plato, Marcus Aurelius Antonius, Dante, Goethe, and two others, neither of them Englishmen, to limbo, as the Seven Humbugs of Christendom. While we are about it, let us leave off talking about 'art for art's sake.' Who is art, that it should have a sake?" (135).

The apprenticeship system must be revived if art is not to die. The secret is in doing one's work with "the affection that attention engenders" (130). He proposes that sketching clubs be formed for people who really want to draw. "The secrets of success," Butler adds, in a passage which tells us much about his own career, "are affection for the pursuit chosen, a flat refusal to be hurried or to pass anything as understood which is not understood, and an obstinacy of character which shall make the student's friends find it less trouble to let him have his own way than to bend him into theirs" (137).

VII *Social and Religious Observations*

A visit to the sanctuary at Oropa leads Butler to some direct speculations regarding the social order. This kind of thing is rare in his works. Here at Oropa a free vacation in the mountains under clean and attractive conditions is offered to the peasantry, much as books and art are offered free in the libraries and galleries of London. Since sleep and a glimpse of comfort are more important to the workingman than books and art, Butler suggests that recreation centers be established in England. He proposes as a start that Oxford and Cambridge be turned into such centers, making them "universities in deed as well as in name" (164-65).

Butler regards "the 'earnestness,' and 'intenseness,' and 'aestheticism,' and 'culture' (for they are in the end one) of the present day" as "so many attempts to conceal weakness" (170). He wishes that moderns could combine the "religious fervour" of Milton and Handel with these artists' ability to appreciate the virtues of paganism. But, he says, this "seems to have become impossible to Protestants since the time of Dr. Arnold" (169). He is convinced that those religions and cultures which are sure of an absolute and eternal standard are so on the surface only. More insight reveals that "nothing is absolutely important or absolutely unimportant, absolutely good or absolutely bad" (174). "We Protestants do not understand, nor take any very great pains to understand, the Church of Rome. If we did, we should find it to be in many respects as much in advance of us as it is behind us in others" (247).

At the religious festival at Locarno, Butler is amused by large American advertisements of a man in a black felt hat smoking a cigarette. "During the illuminations the unwonted light threw its glare upon the effigies of saints and angels, but it illumined also the man in the black felt hat" (248). When the celebrants fell asleep that night on the pavement and under the arches, "the busy persistent vibrations that rise in Anglo-Saxon brains were radiating from every wall, and the man in the black felt hat . . . [was] lying in wait, as a cat over a mouse's hole, to insinuate [himself] into the hearts of the people as soon as they should wake" (248). A prophetic picture for 1881!

Thus *Alps and Sanctuaries* contains many passages of praise for relaxation and good sense: for pilgrims enjoying their pilgrimages, church dignitaries with a sense of humor; for the grace of a life led above the curse of priggishness and affectation.

CHAPTER 8

The Way of All Flesh

I *Background*

BUTLER'S novel, *The Way of All Flesh,* is the best known of
his works. As we have seen, he occupied himself with it off
and on from 1873 to 1885, the year of Miss Savage's death; but it
was not published until 1903. The book owes much to Miss Savage's enthusiasm, to her conviction that Butler could write a novel,
and to her continual urging him on with the work. " 'Never have I
been so calm, so soothed, so happy, so filled with a blessed peace'
etc. as this morning when the first installment of your novel
came," [1] she writes on August 18, 1873. Comments such as the
following, scattered over the years, are the most fully participat-
ing ones which Butler received from anyone concerning his work:
"When am I to have more MS?" [2] (August 30, 1873); "All that I
have read is delightful" [3] (July 20, 1883); "The grand catastrophe
wants vraisemblance.—Your Towneley, too, must be toned down
—a coarse creature with vicious propensities. . . . Ernest gets
tant soit peu priggish—in fact very much so—towards the end,
and especially in the treatment of his children." [4] (November 17,
1883); "I think it is almost perfect this time." [5] (December 2,
1883). Miss Savage projected herself into the novel and lived in
it as Butler wrote it. It is not too much to say that he kept at it
with her delighted response always in mind. When she died, the
audience he loved was gone; he could no longer work on his revision.

Butler had a strong distaste for the popular fiction of his day,
but in his youth he had read widely in Thackeray, Dickens, and
Fielding. Miss Savage urged him to read more novels to learn
how to produce a book that would sell. Under her needling he
read, but for the most part did not enjoy George Eliot's *Middle-
march,* Goethe's *Wilhelm Meister* ("perhaps the very worst book
I ever read" [6]), E. Lynn Linton's *Joshua Davidson,* J. H. Short-

house's *John Inglesant,* Mrs. Ewing's *Jackanapes,* Charles Dudley Warner's *Pusley,* and several Jane Austen novels. He was always an admirer of Disraeli's novels, as he was of the man.

But *The Way of All Flesh* owes more to *Erewhon* and *The Fair Haven* than to any of these writers, and it owes most of all to the kind of man Butler had become by 1880. So true is this that readers temperamentally incapable of sympathizing with Butler are repelled also by his novel and cannot understand why it has been so highly praised. Butler knew about all this. He makes Overton, his narrator, say: "Every man's work, whether it be literature or music or pictures or architecture or anything else, is always a portrait of himself, and the more he tries to conceal himself the more clearly will his character appear in spite of him. I may very likely be condemning myself, all the time that I am writing this book, for I know that whether I like it or no I am portraying myself more surely than I am portraying any of the characters whom I set before the reader" (62).

The Way of All Flesh is a biographical novel about Ernest Pontifex, narrated by Edward Overton, a contemporary of Ernest's father and a friend of the family. It rapidly sketches the lives of Ernest's great-grandfather, a village carpenter, and his grandfather, a successful publisher of religious books, and then gives the life story of his father in some detail. After a fruitless attempt to choose a different occupation, Theobald Pontifex enters the church, marries, and settles down to what Overton reports as a frustrating life as a clergyman, to which profession Theobald is in some respects ill suited. The novel details Ernest's unhappy youth during which he is hounded by both his father and mother; his temporary relief on going to boarding school, only to discover, however, that his masters hound him as his parents had done before; and his intellectual awakening at the university which is characterized by violent extremes of belief. A wealthy aunt had befriended him and had tried her best to give him more robust interests; unfortunately, she dies before her task is accomplished, but she makes him her heir so that he will have security later in life when he has learned the lessons that only life can teach. Ernest, like his father, is destined for the ministry. Under the influence of the revivalist spirit, he is unnaturally anxious to serve the Church; but his very ardor is his undoing.

The sum of money which his aunt leaves him to come to him at once (he knows nothing about his eventual much larger inheritance) is swindled from him by a confidence man acting under the pretense of religious zeal. When Ernest's foolish plans for religious reform tumble about his ears, he switches into extreme skepticism; and, in this mood, he makes the mistake of accosting an honest girl whom in his ignorance he takes for a prostitute. As a consequence, he is thrown in jail. Upon emerging he rejects the help of his parents who are pathetically anxious to bring him back under their influence, marries a woman who had once been a servant in his parents' home, and attempts to establish himself as a tradesman. His wife turns out to be an alcoholic and not his wife at all since she had been previously married. With the help of Overton, Ernest gradually pulls himself out of the ruins of his career, and the novel closes as he comes into his inheritance and enters on a life of public service as a philosophical and critical writer who will tell mankind some of the things about morality, marriage, and the rearing of children which it ought to know.

II *Unaccustomed Angle*

The Way of All Flesh is in many respects the apotheosis in nineteenth-century English fiction of the attempt to view everything from an unaccustomed angle. All novelists indeed must attempt this to some extent to achieve liveliness, but Butler in *The Way of All Flesh* attempts it almost all the time—hence the complaint of bitterness, of coldness, and of biting satire raised against his novel by those who cannot accept the shadow side of life. An example will make clear the point I have in mind. Hidden beneath the surface of every marriage, under the publicly accepted features, is the obverse side of exploitation, fear, mistrust, and shock, even though sentimental people refuse to admit this. To have a wedding described in terms of these hidden features appalls those who accept the public facade as the only reality. Mr. Heatherley's reactions are typical. Butler tells us that he "said I had taken all the tenderest feelings of our nature and, having spread them carefully over the floor, stamped upon them till I had reduced them to an indistinguishable mass of filth . . . I do not take this view of the matter myself." [7] Like Butler, we too must not take this view.

Since the unexpected makes us laugh, if it does not repel us, the opening part of *The Way of All Flesh* strikes readers as uproariously funny. Butler indeed wanted it to do so. Like all real humor, however, it is tragic as well as funny—and sometimes we do not know whether to laugh or to weep at this surprisingly inverse but convincing world to which we are introduced. The events in the early story of Theobald's university life, for example, his engagement to Christina Allaby, his marriage, and his ministry are vividly portrayed; but simultaneously they are mercilessly exposed in the light of a higher kind of wisdom. A letter proposing marriage is generally a touching thing, but Butler concludes Theobald's letter to Christina with the comment: "And this was all that his public school and University education had been able to do for Theobald!" (47). Theobald's father, on hearing of his son's engagement, might have been portrayed as an injured parent for whom we should feel sorry. Instead, our narrator comments that the occasion "afforded a golden opportunity which the old gentleman . . . embraced with characteristic eagerness" (49). What a shock to learn that vindictiveness is something we enjoy! Hardly a page of the novel presents events in their ordinary light. Rather than bitterness, what is operating in it is a greater perceptiveness than we are accustomed to. This the reader must see, or he cannot comprehend *The Way of All Flesh.*

Right from the start, we discover that we are in unusual hands. Old Mr. Pontifex, a mediocre failure from the ordinary point of view, is described in terms that suggest his preeminent success as a human being: " 'We must judge men not so much by what they do,' " Edward Overton's father tells him, " 'as by what they make us feel that they have it in them to do' " (4-5). This is a mildly romantic inversion of values. But it is only a beginning. George Pontifex's very human admiration for accepted classics— the St. Gotthard Pass, the Uffizi Gallery—is treated with scorn on the grounds that his reactions come from no true feelings of his own. Then money and children are compared, with children coming out on the short end—money is "never naughty," does not "spill things on the tablecloth at meal time." Can it be that, deep within us, we too resent children as George unconsciously does? "How little do we know our thoughts," Butler says, in a chapter put together by his literary executor from his notes, ". . . it is our less conscious thoughts and our less conscious actions which mainly mold our lives and the lives of those who spring from us" (22). This is the program for his novel—to reveal the hidden and obverse. Here is no Erewhonian phantasyland, no Italy of one's dreams, but the very world we ourselves live in subjected to a prophetic reevaluation.

III *Transvaluation of All Values*

The subversive view of morality which pervades the entire novel, whereby the traditionally virtuous becomes evil and the evil virtuous, comes before us in passage after passage and event after event and is the most striking feature of the book. One critic speculates that Butler is defending the view of life of the English lower classes and of the highest aristocracy in opposition to middle-class morality, and thus is initiating a new trend in the novel which led directly to D. H. Lawrence's later works.[8] There is truth in this view, but in a sense it is coincidental. Butler wrote this way not through a sentimental attachment for the underdog but because he was deeply convinced that the happiness of mankind demanded a transvaluation of all values. Mr. Allaby, a rector with nine children and an income of only £600 a year, would normally be admired by the middle class for his spiritual, self-sacrificing life. Butler comments about anyone who could get himself into such a predicament: "If morality is that which, on the whole, brings a man peace in his declining years—if, that is to say, it is not an utter swindle, can you under these circumstances flatter yourself that you have led a moral life? . . . Someone should do for morals what that old Pecksniff Bacon has obtained the credit of having done for science" (37).

Traditionally, we admire a parent who has his children well educated. Butler observes about George Pontifex who tried to accomplish this result: "He did not see that the education cost the children far more than it cost him, inasmuch as it cost them the power of earning their living easily . . . and ensured their being at the mercy of their father for years" (24). He finds the church catechism wanting: "I should like to introduce a few words insisting on the duty of seeking all reasonable pleasure and avoiding all pain that can be honourably avoided" (31). And the scorching light thrown upon the harmful effects of a silly religiosity in the recurrent daydreams of Christina, bordering as they do on mania, is excruciating; the knife of the skillful surgeon is at work here, cutting away what desperately needs to be removed. " 'We, dearest Theobald,' " she exclaims, " 'will be ever faithful. We will stand firm and support one another even in the hour of death itself. God in his mercy may spare us from being burnt alive. . . . O Lord . . . spare my Theobald, or grant that he may be beheaded.'" Whereupon Theobald replies: "'Such a life let us pray God that it may please Him to enable us to pray that we may lead.'" "The moon had risen," Butler concludes this episode, "and the arbour was getting damp, so they adjourned further aspirations for a more convenient season" (53). Immediately after his marriage Theobald's real self protests the trap which deference to tradition has sprung upon him: "He didn't mean to have married Christina; he hadn't married her; it was all a hideous dream; he would— But a voice kept ringing in his ears which said: 'YOU CAN'T, CAN'T, CAN'T.' 'CAN'T I?' screamed the unhappy creature to himself. 'NO,' said the remorseless voice, 'YOU CAN'T. YOU ARE A MARRIED MAN'" (58).

IV Stream-of-Consciousness Technique

In developing the portrait of Christina, Butler makes use of a device he had begun to use in *The Fair Haven* to present the daydreams of John Pickard Owen's mother. It is a forerunner of the stream-of-consciousness technique used by later novelists, so many of whom were influenced by *The Way of All Flesh*. "For Ernest a very great future—she was certain of it—was in store. . . . Heaven would bear her witness that she had never shrunk from the idea of martyrdom for herself and Theobald, nor would she avoid it for her boy, if his life was required of her in her Redeemer's service. Oh, no! . . . It was not for nothing that Ernest had been baptized in water from the Jordan. . . . Why, it was a miracle! It was! It was! She saw it all now. The Jordan had left its bank and flowed into her own house. . . . And so on for hours together day after day for years" (89-91). These daydreams occur again and again in the novel, culminating in a final glorious one as Christina is dying and sees Ernest in Parliament, made Prime Minister, raised to the peerage as Lord Battersby, and herself immortalized in a famous "Portrait of Lord Battersby's Mother,"— "and so on till her daughter told her it was time to take her medicine" (373-74).

V   *Truth to Oneself and Revolt*

The locus of the transvaluation presented in *The Way of All Flesh* is partly in the need for moderation. "The greatest and wisest of mankind will be almost always found to be the meanest —the ones who have kept the 'mean' best between excess either of virtue or vice" (83). But even more, the locus is in the requirement of being true to oneself. " 'You are surrounded on every side by lies,' " Ernest's real self says to him, " 'which would deceive even the elect, if the elect were not generally so uncommonly wide awake; the self of which you are conscious, your reasoning and reflecting self, will believe these lies and bid you act in accordance with them. This conscious self of yours, Ernest, is a prig begotten of prigs and trained in priggishness; I will not allow it to shape your actions. . . . Obey *me*, your true self, and things will go tolerably well with you, but only listen to that outward and visible husk of yours which is called your father, and I will rend you in pieces even unto the third and fourth generation as one who has hated God; for I, Ernest, am the God who made you' " (131).

The Way of All Flesh is a study of revolt and, even more, of the danger of failure to revolt. It covers five generations to illustrate Butler's theories of inheritance. But more important, it shows the enduring effects of revolt and revenge; and it makes the point unforgettably clear by iteration. Spanning the whole story is Edward Overton, the narrator and commentator—in a sense Butler himself—who from the start shows himself capable of genuine insight into the meaning of the tragedies which unfold. The figure of old Mr. Pontifex, the carpenter, kindly, unassuming, capable, stands at the start as the picture of what mankind can achieve. In a way he is the novel's hero as its most perfect man[9]—Pontifex, the bridgemaker. We remember that Jesus, too, was a carpenter. Pontifex's disciplining of his servant epitomizes the way in which the older generation should deal with the younger. Readers who call this novel merely destructive seem to have skipped this important material. Edward has come to Mr. Pontifex to get some glue—the stuff of adhesion—when he witnesses the hope-giving scene. The desire for revenge is the result of failure to revolt; three generations after old Mr. Pontifex are cursed by the injuries done to them by the fathers; and only the fourth, Ernest's, has the courage to refuse the way of revenge, the handing on of the curse. It is not without interest to remember that Dostoevsky in Russia was writing his masterpiece on this same subject, *The Brothers Karamazov*, during the years that Butler worked on *The Way of All Flesh*. Dostoevsky's novel spans fewer generations, but in the four brothers it compresses into one generation the variety Butler spreads over five. His Ivan, like Ernest, tries to find his way out of his tragedy by writing and philosophizing, though he does not comprehend the importance of faith as Ernest comes to do. This insight is left to Alyosha.

VI *Story of the Generations*

Each of the generations in *The Way of All Flesh* is portrayed with increasing detail. Old Pontifex comes first in a few idyllic chapters, casting the nostalgic charm of the old village way of life over the novel's opening, with details chosen to underline the self-fulfillment of this carpenter-artist-musician who loved everyone and was in turn beloved, and who said goodbye to the sun just before his death. More space is devoted to his successful son George as the story moves closer to its center. He is well educated, travels abroad, and enters the business world in London, leaving the country for the city. How explain the evil that really begins with him? Butler deals in no melodramatic villains and heroes in his novel—his insight is too penetrating for such simplification. Perhaps George had risen too rapidly in life to be sure of himself; perhaps he was a throwback to a previous ancestor, or was more like his mother than his father. In any case, taken all in all, he was a successful man: "Having lived to be nearly seventy-three years old and died rich he must have been in very fair harmony with his surroundings. . . . The psalmist says, 'The righteous shall not lack anything that is good.' Either this is mere poetical licence, or it follows that he who lacks anything that is good is not righteous. . . . [George] Pontifex never lacked anything he much cared about" (81-82).

But George is not the man his father was. George shows no compunction about lying in the presence of Gelstrap, his servant, who knows he is lying. Worst of all, he is a master at torturing his children under the impression that he is doing them good. Yet again Butler observes, "It shows no great moral obliquity on the part of parents if within certain limits they make their children's lives a burden to them" (83). The evil does seem to come, though, from those whom Overton understands and to an extent even forgives, who tolerate and encourage will-shaking, useless educations, browbeating of children, and from men who do not know the art of being themselves.

Theobald, George's son and the chief victim of his aggressiveness and cruelty, has more space and detail devoted to his portraiture. His story represents the third stage in the fivefold novel. Theobald has cause to revolt, but he unconsciously and in conformity with accepted patterns chooses the path of revenge, doing unto his children as had been done unto him—only more so. A glimmer of resistance flickers when he audaciously proposes to his father that he not enter the ministry. But George subdues him with one blow: "'You shall not receive a single six-pence from me till you come to your senses'" (35). Theobald surrenders.

VII *Basis in Reality*

Butler has been accused of caricaturing his own father in the portrait of Theobald. Significantly, he wrote to his sister May on November 12, 1873, after he had begun the book, that he had written no work drawing on any living person, and would never do so.[10] Obviously, however, Theobald's abortive revolt and Ernest's real one are both patterned on Butler's own. And so many other details of the Theobald Pontifex family life are drawn directly from Butler's youth, including the letter taken verbatim from one his mother wrote for him and his brother,[11] that no one can deny that the novel has much basis in reality. But so do all the great novels of the nineteenth century and many of the twentieth. The point, though, is that the artistic duplication of events, the arrangement, and the meaning are poetic creations and not slavish transcripts. It is surely a mistake, as Arnold Silver points out,[12] to regard Ernest as merely a portrait of the author, or Theobald as merely a portrait of the author's father.

VIII *The Heart of the Story*

The story of Theobald is told briefly, succinctly, acidly. We should remember if we are repelled by it that in many respects it is the same as the story of Ernest which, beginning with Chapter 20, will be told in fuller detail and with greater warmth. Neither story is complete without the other. In the second telling there is more sympathy and understanding, more of the complex vision of many points of view; and the whole is much closer to what we expect of a novel. Still, the sharp inversions of the Theobald story have already taught us their lesson, and we are always aware, having learned it, that the truth is not what it appears to be. We have been shocked into a double vision in spite of ourselves. Theobald does his best in bringing up his son to adhere to the standards of his day, and it is only from the standpoint of this double vision that we may see him as cruel, dishonest, and cowardly. With the exception of Overton, Theobald's children, the butler John, Mrs. Jupp, Alethea, and perhaps the reader of the novel, everyone regards Theobald as a perfect man, underlining the fact that he is doing what the world expects: "He was beloved by all who had anything to do with him." And Butler adds, "The general verdict is often the truest" (403). Is the whole society condemned, or is Theobald justified? This question the reader must answer for himself.

IX *Ernest—a Hero?*

Ernest, Theobald's son, the fourth generation and the novel's central character, is only heroic if we respond to him as Overton and Butler and the double vision compel us to. Otherwise, he is so weak, ungrateful, and selfish that he is repelling and not worth reading about. How, we may ask, can any human being worth his salt be as foolish as Ernest is? But—Butler and Overton and our new vision force us to ask—does not his weakness arise from his tragically wrong upbringing, and is it not a miracle that he survives with a will of his own at all and is not submerged into what his parents want him to become? Is it not surprising that he has enough individuality to interest his Aunt Alethea in him, and eventually to power his revolt? The hero is there, but unrecognizable, hidden—a hero who after long defeat and frustration will ultimately turn on his tormentors. We find the basic allegory true and powerful—more powerful than the story of a man of obvious fighting qualities, and more powerful than if Ernest had scored an open success. This is the story of an underdog, but one made meaningful through compassion and understanding.

We follow Ernest through his pathetic youth—"Before Ernest could well crawl he was taught to kneel; before he could well speak he was taught to lisp the Lord's prayer. . . ." (88)—and

are touched by his desire to love all things that will allow him to
be fond of them. "It was long," Butler tells us, before his mother
"could destroy all affection for herself in the mind of her first-
born. But she persevered" (89). After he had beaten Ernest for
saying "Tum" rather than "Come," Theobald said, "'And now,
Christina, I think we will have the servants in to prayers,' and he
rang the bell for them, red-handed as he was" (96). The pres-
sures toward parricide are building up—the word "red-handed"
has connotations of real bloodshed.[13]

X *Attempted Rescue*

Ernest's experiences at Dr. Skinner's Roughborough Grammar
School add little happiness to his life. Dr. Skinner is a hypocrite
of the first water, though even he can be admired for being so
solidly what he is. And Ernest remains weak, pathetic, and afraid.
Here a fairy godmother, that device so dear to the Victorian heart,
enters the story in Aunt Alethea, the character Butler modeled on
Miss Savage, to build up Ernest's ego by giving him money and
affection. She shares Overton's wisdom; she knows that Ernest
can be strengthened if he is allowed "to kiss the soil" (291)—a
Tolstoian touch! She arranges for him to have carpentry lessons
and asks him to build an organ for her.

Alethea gives him the love and affection his real mother should
have given him. When Alethea dies, she leaves her estate to Ernest without his knowledge, to come to him when he is twenty-
eight. Some readers say that Ernest's being provided for in this
fashion makes the novel ineffective. But Ernest does not know
that he will be saved financially, and by the time he gets his estate he has proved himself sufficiently without it. Obviously, he
could have made his way by then, money or no money. Overton
would certainly have helped him at crucial moments. Ernest is
not overprotected, and this is not the typical fairy godmother of
Gilbert and Sullivan, who appears from nowhere in the closing
scene.

XI *The Tragedy of Sex*

An important theme of the novel, implicit in the story of the
courtship of Theobald and Christina and explicit in the story of
Ernest, is the tragic effect of a completely unrealistic attitude toward sex. The attractive eighteen-year-old Ellen, servant in the

rectory at Battersby, is dismissed instantly when she is found to be pregnant. Christina fears—and half hopes—that Ernest may be the father of the child, but neither she nor Theobald dares discuss the question openly, though one of the harrowing "sofa sessions" is devoted to it. This fumbling lays the groundwork for the disastrous encounter with Miss Maitland which lands Ernest in jail, and it leads directly to Ernest's final revolt.

Many touches show that this bungling within the family is not quaint and harmless but deadly dangerous. Theobald prepares Ernest for a trap in connection with a missing watch in true Federal Bureau of Investigation style: " 'Oh, Ernest,' said he, in an offhand, rather cheery manner, 'there's a little matter which I should like you to explain to me . . .' Thump, thump, thump, went Ernest's heart against his ribs" (177). "It never occured to Ernest to ask his father why he did not hit a man his own size" (179). When John, the butler, stands up to Theobald, he backs down immediately, coward that he is. Later the real third degree begins. Ernest tries to protect his schoolfellows, but "the thumb-screws were instantly applied. . . . He was examined, re-examined, cross-examined, sent to the retirement of his own bedroom and cross-examined again . . . and yet Theobald had on the preceding Sunday preached a less feeble sermon than he commonly preached, upon the horrors of the Inquisition. . . . The pair never flinched, but probed and probed, till they were on the point of reaching subjects more delicate than they had yet touched upon. Here Ernest's unconscious self took the matter up and made a resistance to which his conscious self was unequal, by tumbling him off his chair in a fit of fainting" (184-85). Throughout the novel, Butler reminds us that psychic tortures affect the body. Ernest goes through illnesses and breakdown, just as do John Pickard Owen and Higgs.

XII *The Failure of Education*

The basic futility of Ernest's education at Cambridge is skillfully hinted at in the account of the prayer meeting in the rooms of the Simeonites at which Mr. Hawke's eloquent and adept manipulation of his audience hoodwinks Ernest completely; sweeps him, a senior about to graduate, quite off his feet; and prepares him for ordination, against which even his father had momentarily rebelled. So ardently does Ernest's religious fervor flame up that even his father is frightened. The young man is far from knowing what he really wants from life. Then follows the disgraceful episode in which he allows Pryer to manipulate him, to get his money from him, to persuade him to embark on a complete reform of the Church, and generally to drive him toward chaos. Has he no stability at all?

The climax and turning point comes with his arrest and with his decision to break with his past. These are artfully led up to by his encounter with Mr. Shaw, who in a few words shows him that he knows nothing about the Bible; by his hearing Towneley, his hero, say " 'No, no, no' " (254) to his whole way of life; and by his reading of the *Vestiges of Creation*. In prison Ernest has an attack of brain fever, but on recovery he is given the only real education he ever had and learns to be a tailor. Does one have to go to jail to become educated? On his discharge, Theobald and Christina are at the prison gate to receive him. " 'We must never leave him to himself' " Theobald says, and Christina adds, " 'Our voices [will be] the first to exhort him to return to the paths of virtue' " (301).

Ernest was as white as a sheet. His heart beat so that he could hardly breathe. . . . Then, gathering strength, he said . . . 'Mother, . . . we must part.' . . . Theobald stepped forward. 'Ernest, you must not, shall not, leave us in this way.' 'Do not speak to me' said Ernest, his eyes flashing with a fire that was unwonted in them. . . . 'Tell them [he said to the Warden] from me that they must think of me as one dead, for I am dead to them.' . . . After he had got a few steps out he turned his face to the prison wall, leant against it for support, and wept as though his heart would break.   (302-03)

XIII   *The Making of a Man*

The road upward from his degradation and revolt is not easy for Ernest, even though Overton stands in the background ready to help. His ignorance of life has not yet taken its full toll. He marries Ellen—illegally, it turns out, since she was already married ("I think the devil must have chuckled and made tolerably sure of his game this time" (315) Butler comments). Two children are born; but Ernest is so inexperienced that he does not discover that Ellen is an alcoholic. When at last he is freed from her, the movement upward begins.

The resolution of the novel has often been criticized. Butler never revised the last part as he had intended to, and it is therefore long and discursive; it needs tightening. But the central theme is unmistakable. Ernest wishes to become a philosophical writer who by his writings will help mankind to better itself, to avoid the mistakes he has made. Significantly, his first big project is to gather information about the marriage customs of many races, to ascertain which people are the happiest, and to report his findings to his countrymen. This does not mean that he has become a little Samuel Butler, or that his career peters out into futility and pettiness. The great Victorian literary tradition held that the writer is a cultural leader. Butler was scornful of men like Carlyle and Arnold because he rejected their premises, but he was not scornful of literature as a dialogue carried on with vigor, honesty, and skill. Our contemporary conviction that the artist—whether he be novelist, poet, or dramatist—can be more effective than the philosophical writer, essayist, even journalist, is not necessarily the right one.[14] Perhaps Ernest is no more futile in his dedication than Stephen Dedalus in his. In his great vision of the future, *Das Glasperlenspiel*, Hermann Hesse sees our period as one of journalism. Why should not men like Ernest contribute to the future creatively, just as Butler tried to do?

Of course, if the reader expects Ernest to emerge from his valley a conquering hero, to find a beautiful mate, and to fall into the traditional pattern of the wealthy English gentleman, he will be disappointed. In the light of his experience of fathers and sons, Ernest settles his parental problem at one stroke by paying a healthy, simple couple to bring up his children. Given what Butler has told us about family life, who can say that he was wrong? The results, we are informed, are most fortunate. The fifth generation recaptures the instinctive happiness that the first one possessed. Ernest's daughter marries happily, with none of the "wurra-wurra" of Mrs. Allaby, and his son moves into a prosperous profession with none of the troubles of his father. This is not heroic; but, in terms of what the novel has presented, it makes good sense indeed. And Ernest slowly forges ahead, though he has things to say that his contemporaries do not want to hear; and so he must expect to remain an outsider for the present. His hope, like his creator's, is for future acceptance.

While in prison Ernest had not only learned how to be a good tailor; he had also dropped his belief in Christian supernaturalism, and he had done some pondering on the nature of truth. If, he thought, "Truth is what commends itself to the great majority of sensible and successful people" (282), were there no exceptions? Could not the sensible majority on occasion be wrong? He concluded that on some matters, instinct must be the court of appeal, and that the just must live by faith. Faith, and not reason, is the *ultima ratio*. His hope, then, was to save through his writings "the hundreds and thousands of young people throughout England whose lives were being blighted through the lies told them by people whose business it was to know better, but who scamped their work and shirked difficulties instead of facing them." He wanted to save "others from such years of waste and misery as he had had to pass himself" (284).

The course Ernest charts out is similar to the course Butler charted out: he begins by abortive attempts to write for magazines and newspapers; he adopts evolution as an article of faith (364); he decides to stir up the hornets' nest of marriage and the family system (388); he publishes a volume "of semi-theological, semi-social essays, purporting to have been written by six or seven different people, and viewing the same class of subjects from different standpoints" (393); and finally he gets himself a bad literary character because of his capacity for making trouble. But he is unperturbed by lack of success, for he feels he is addressing the next generation. All he says is " 'Wait' " (410). None of this, of course, is at all spectacular. There are no shouts of applause, no heroic posing at the novel's end. The victory is an internal one, and cannot be overtly dramatized, though it is nonetheless real. With the kindly help of Overton—and who is to say we are not to help each other in this life?—Ernest has become his own man—not another Overton, not another Butler, but, in his own fashion, a builder of bridges into an uncertain, nebulous future.

CHAPTER 9

Carrying On

I *The "Earnest Clergyman"*

WITH the manuscript of his most important work unpublished,[1] Butler turned to a variety of other projects in his continuing attempt to speak to his era. These included, as we have seen, his books on evolution. During the spring of 1879 he published under various pseudonyms a series of letters in the *Examiner*. In them he carefully developed several conflicting points of view about the dilemma of a clergyman who is supposed, after having studied *Essays and Reviews*, Bishop Colenso, and Darwin,[2] to have become a skeptic. This "Earnest Clergyman" writes the first two letters. He is middle-aged, married, has five children, and has no way of earning a living if he leaves his post. What is he to do?

"Cantab." writes the third letter in the series. He points out that no one should be blamed for not being heroic, since heroism is exceptional behavior. He therefore urges the "Earnest Clergyman" to stick to his post, saying that even though the "Clergyman" rejects some church doctrines, he can work on the practical, moral level and make a worthy contribution to the cause of a better life. To this the "Clergyman" replies that he wants to be neither too far ahead nor too far behind the average man, but he cannot base his life upon a fiction. A third letter writer, "Oxoniensis," now appears who attacks the "cultured scepticism" of "Cantab." and states categorically that Christianity, being divine, is either all true in every detail or nothing but a fraud. No self-respecting man, he argues, can remain a minister unless he believes wholly and absolutely in the doctrine of his church. A fourth debater, "Ethics," thereupon states his conviction that it is better to deceive others knowing that we are doing so, as the "Earnest Clergyman" is doing, than to deceive ourselves as "Cantab." has urged. He gives examples of animals and plants which make their living by deception, and he says that the individual man cannot settle the great questions of his life for himself, but must do what he is called upon to do.

"Cantab." defends himself by drawing a distinction between the divine truth, which must be perfect, and the limited truth, which is all that man knows. On the basis of this latter truth man can work in the practical sphere, even if he rejects some of it. "Oxoniensis" immediately attacks this distinction, calling it unmanly and fraudulent; but "Cantab." replies that it is irrational to say that Christianity is either all right or all wrong. The question to be raised is: What can *we* know to be true?

After "Ethics" writes to agree with "Cantab.," a fifth writer, "Lewis Wright," points out that all men must lie to some extent. What is the fisherman but a liar when he disguises his hook with a worm? The thirteenth contribution to the series is Butler's poem "The Righteous Man," signed "X.Y.Z." In this poem he holds up to scorn those who do good only when force is on their side. Then the "Earnest Clergyman" rejects the views of both "Cantab." and "Oxoniensis" as too extreme; he argues that the crucial requirement in all such matters is to avoid the shock that comes from pushing too fast and too far. The exchange, in which Butler practices some of the debating of issues built into the substance of *The Way of All Flesh*, concludes with two letters from other clergymen both of whom describe themselves as caught in the dilemma of the "Earnest Clergyman" and who warn young men thinking of the ministry to take heed before it is too late. "E.D." says, "I wish to save some from the mental torture which I have endured" (*Collected Essays*, I, 98), and "Sollicitus" adds, "Earnestly would I join with 'E.D.' in exhorting young men thinking of orders to pause, or they may find themselves in evil case in after years" (99).

There can be little doubt that one of the deepest motives behind the writing of *The Way of All Flesh* was Butler's desire to present some of the tragedies and injustices of life with such vividness that future generations might avoid needless suffering. In the dramatic exchange of letters we have just reviewed, his aim is the same; and the concluding two epistles drive home the point. The argument is fought out cleverly and clearly. None of the writers is given an obvious victory, any more than are any of the proponents in the multivoiced *Fair Haven*. The whole exchange stands as a warning, as an appeal to use intelligence and open-eyed awareness. And yet Butler had strong personal convictions. Even in the days of *The Fair Haven* his conscious mind was clear about which view he subscribed to,[3] and as late as 1887 he wrote to a friend: "Till Christianity is dead and buried we shall never get the burning questions that lie beyond approached in a spirit of sobriety and commonsense. It is therefore against superstition, and more especially the Christian superstition, that I have fought to the best of my ability."[4] But intuition told him that these convictions were best served when, as in these letters and in his novel, he presented them in complex form. Which of the letter-writers wins out? That depends on the reader, though at the least the fact that there is something real to debate emerges crystal clear; and the reader may be persuaded unawares.

II *"God the Known and God the Unknown"*

Following this exchange of letters, the *Examiner* in May, June, and July of 1879 published a series of articles which Butler called "God the Known and God the Unknown." In these he attempts to become definite about the possible theological implications of his *Life and Habit* theory. The articles do less than justice to the subtlety of his mind, however, and lack the suggestive and imaginative power of his books of this period. Although passages in the *Note-Books* develop the ideas here set forth, it is hard to believe that Butler is as sure of himself as he pretends to be.

Briefly put, Butler's argument goes as follows. Given the identity of all life to which his theory of memory led, each living being can be thought of as a part of the known God. We ourselves thus are God, and He exists and expresses Himself through us. This known God can arouse real emotion. Butler writes:

The theologian dreams of a God sitting above the clouds among the cherubim, who blow their loud uplifted angel trumpets before Him, and humor Him as though He were some despot in an Oriental tale; but we enthrone Him upon the wings of birds, on the petals of flowers, on the faces of our friends, and upon whatever we most delight in of all that lives upon the earth. We then can not only love Him, but we can do that without which love has neither power nor sweetness, but is a phantom only, an impersonal person, a vain stretching forth of arms towards something that can never fill them—we can express our love and have it expressed to us in return. And this not in the uprearing of stone temples—for the Lord dwelleth in temples made with other organs than hands—nor yet in the cleansing of our hearts, but in the caress bestowed upon horse and dog, and kisses upon the lips of those we love. (*Collected Essays*, I, 37-38)

There is eloquence to this, perhaps even truth. But to explain the origin of this known God in whom we participate, Butler goes on to say that we may imagine a greater unknown God of whom the known God is a part as each cell is a part of us. This transcendent God at which he thus arrives seems distant, unreal, and little better than the Gods of the pantheist or the anthropomorphist which he rejects. The argument bogs down in the materialistic cause-and-effect thinking of his era which Butler, at his best, rose above. It simply is not capable of bearing the emotional and theological weight he attempts to put upon it. Emerson and Thoreau might have understood and sympathized with his known God; they would have rejected the matter-of-fact reasoning leading to the unknown God. Significantly, Butler never republished these articles, and he never again tried to set forth so definite a theology.

III *Whistling in the Dark*

In 1886, as we have seen, Canon Butler died and Butler's financial problems were finally resolved. He now had more than enough money to meet his needs. He "bought a pair of new hair brushes and a larger wash-hand basin";[5] he soon hired Alfred Emery Cathie to be his clerk, valet, and secretary; and he allowed Henry Festing Jones a stipend to enable him to spend more time working with him. A subtle change took place in Butler as he grew older and more secure. With his best work either unpublished or, when published, vilified (even though a few words of praise were heard from time to time), he had won no real audience and had been operating pretty much in a vacuum. His tendency toward elaborate pretense of scorn for the opinion of others, his strong conviction that an artist must do what he wants to do no matter what people say, had slowly become a mode of whistling in the dark. There is no doubt that he gradually adopted a kind of bravado to shield himself from the subtle corrections which, as he well knew, reality forces upon the healthy organism. No elaborate inner explanation needs to be sought for the maladjustment which grew more noticeable in him from this time on—the slightly ridiculous world of good fellowship he built up with Jones, Cathie, and a small circle of friends; the somewhat exaggerated fussiness about his various theories; and the odd causes he championed. The explanation is at hand in the absence of a proper "loading factor" in the form of a critical and appreciative audience for what he did.

All this is not to say that the work of Butler's concluding period was negligible. Even in these final sixteen years, his writing remains interesting and provocative, and he continues to evince a remarkable measure of sanity and imagination. But his conviction that the polite, cultured self-satisfaction of the established groups of his day, especially of the scientists and scholars, was a monumental sham became sharper and sharper as the years passed, right up to the end of his life. As time went on, he was to make things harder for the few of his contemporaries who attended to him and for those of us who read him now. It is as though he were taking revenge for his lonely position and crying out, "Just see if you can agree with me!" [6]

IV *Running a Theory*

When Butler wrote *Alps and Sanctuaries,* he did not discuss Varallo-Sesia, in his opinion the most important of the north Italian sanctuaries, because, as he stated, it deserved a book to itself. He now wrote that book—*Ex Voto,* published in 1888. The view that Jones gives us of what Butler was doing is discouraging. Writing to Butler's artist friend, Charles Gogin, from Varallo which he and Butler were visiting, he says: "He has been making great progress with a new Italian book which is to run this place and Gaudenzio Ferrari. . . . There is another man who did statues up here, Tabachetti, who is also to be run." [7]

Butler had long felt that many learned men and scholars had built their reputations on the unscrupulous "running" of a theory, a more or less well-known figure, or a pet project in which he could hardly think that they believed. He was convinced that they were simply getting all the percentage they could from a special racket. Leaving aside the question of how consciously or unconsciously this was done, the idea makes a good satirical point about the ways of the learned world. The irony in this, however, is that apparently Butler is about to do the same thing he thought the professionals did. Does the "running" remain a game

to him, in the spirit of Hesse's *Das Glasperlenspiel;* or is he, like
the learned savants, to take it as his own private racket? Jones'
remark suggests coldbloodedness. This can hardly have been the
heart of the matter, but at the least the phrasing of Jones' comment suggests that the idea probably came from Butler himself.[8]

All the paraphernalia of *Ex Voto* indicate complete seriousness
on Butler's part—the endless hours of research in libraries and
museums in preparing his book, the search for early sources, the
careful documentation, the elaborate quarrels with experts in the
field. Indeed, in this and in following works Butler revealed
the shortcomings, errors, and lack of scholarly care in those with
whom he differed by bearing down with savage skill on specific
points. His analysis in *Ex Voto* of Sir Henry Layard's discussion
of Varallo is a good example (2-6); it stands comparison with
Lessing's *Vademekum für Herrn Lange.* Yet, in general, the structure he proceeds to erect in the place of what he demolishes is
not much more satisfactory than the demolished one; for he in-
evitably leaves many new loopholes open. It is an exciting and
endless game, if game it really is.

V   Ex Voto

The Sacri Monte at Varallo was neglected and run down; but,
when Butler first visited it in 1871[9] and when he visited it again
on many subsequent occasions, he was impressed by the beauty
and naturalness of the Biblical figures in the chapels there. Perhaps they spoke to a hidden longing in him to have the world of
traditional religion which he had rejected come to life in spite of
himself. In any case, he became convinced that "Tabachetti's
Journey to Calvary . . . is of such superlative excellence as regards composition and dramatic power, to say nothing of the
many admirable individual figures comprised in it, that it is not
too much to call it the most astounding work that has ever been
achieved in sculpture" (62). Other complex forces working behind this "discovery" may have been Butler's instinctive sympathy for the outcast and unrecognized—derived from his awareness of his own position as an Ishmael—and his abiding desire to
make discoveries in which no one else could claim a part.[10] An
additional factor might be that "it drove its unhappy creator mad,
which the Medicean chapel never did by Michael Angelo" (62).

Butler had bought two cameras, had taken some lessons in photography, and had spent many hours photographing the statues at Varallo. The pictures in his book do a good deal to help the reader understand his discussion, and they show also that he was not wrong to be enthusiastic about these figures. Caiaphas, for example, and St. Joseph are remarkable characterizations, masterfully executed. Il Vecchiotto, which he regarded as "perhaps the finest figure of all, who looks as if he had dropped straight from the heavens," (63) is not so impressive, unless one thinks of him as an embodiment of old John Pontifex!

One of Butler's primary aims in writing *Ex Voto* is again to persuade the reader to look upon art with his own eyes—not with the eyes of tradition. In his enthusiasm for the modest and unassuming he leans toward what in our time would be called a taste for the primitive. The opening chapters contain some excellent suggestions for acquiring a fresher, more spontaneous view of art. Butler likes Tabachetti more than Gaudenzio Ferrari because he had "a robustness, and freedom from mannerism and self-repetition, that are not always observable in Gaudenzio's work" (83). But there is a danger in his application of his own lesson. So enamored does he become of his insights that he convinces himself that every statue at Varallo and in the neighborhood which is unusually beautiful must be the work of Tabachetti, the master of them all; and he proceeds to build a castle of inferences upon his subjective preference. He draws, too, upon his own practices as a writer in assuming that striking portraits must be based on living beings and that he can detect resemblances to real people. Thus he finds three portraits of Tabachetti himself, two of Leonardo da Vinci, and two of Stefano Scotti.

Butler's feelings about greatness in art are presented as follows:

With few exceptions even the best art-work falls into one of two classes, and offers signs either of immaturity or decline. . . . Michael Angelo said the last word; but then he said just a word or two over. So with Titian and Leonardo da Vinci, and in music with Haydn, Mozart, and Beethoven. We . . . feel the presence of an autumnal tint over all the luxuriance of development which . . . tells of an art that has taken not an upward but a downward path. . . . It is only with the very few, as with Homer and Shakespeare at their best . . . and in music with Handel, that I can see no step left unclimbed, yet none taken on the downward path. (181)

Later, he speculates about the fickleness of fame: "We flatter ourselves that among the kings and queens of art, music, and literature, or at any rate in the kingdom of the great dead, all wrongs shall be redressed, and patient merit shall take no more quips and scorns from the unworthy. . . . It is not so. . . . The reputations of the great dead . . . are governed in the main by the chicane that obtains among the living" (201). Yet Butler recognizes that art must die: "How is it to end if we go on at our present rate, with huge geological formations of art and book middens accreting in every city of Europe? Who is to see them, who even to catalogue them? . . . With such a surfeit of art and science the mind palls and longs to be relieved from both. . . . Let [a man's work] live in the use which passeth all praise or thanks or even understanding, and let the story die after a certain time as all things else must do" (203-04).

In concluding his work, Butler generalizes about religion. "I, and those who think as I do, would see the letter whether of science or of Christianity made less of, and the spirit more. Slowly, but very slowly . . . things move in this direction" (211). But "that the letter of the coming faith will be greatly truer than that of the many that have preceded it," he adds, "I for one do not believe. . . . I would as soon have a winking Madonna . . . as the doubtful experiments . . . which the high priests of modern science are applauded with one voice for trying to palm off upon their devotees" (213). His final hope is that "the work of the just men made perfect through suffering that have gone before" (214) will ease the lot of mankind.

The *Spectator*[11] reviewed *Ex Voto* at length, calling it a "singular book" with "vivid descriptions" and "strange and fascinating illustrations." "Its startling ideas," the reviewer says, "amounting often to discoveries and new departures in the world of religious art—its criticisms, full of knowledge and originality, if also of a certain mocking spirit which destroys the effect of it for some minds—this book, with all its peculiarities, is certainly a striking contribution to literature of the kind."

VI *Articles on Art*

In 1886 Butler published in *The Athenaeum* (February 20 and May 15) two articles on "Portraits of Gentile and Giovanni Bellini" (*Collected Essays*, II, 151-56) in which he attempted to defend the genuineness of a Louvre painting which had recently been ascribed to Cariani. He noted the age of the previously accepted tradition that the picture was by Gentile Bellini, and also expressed his belief that the same two heads appeared in the Bellini picture "St. Mark's Sermon," in a fresco by Titian, and in Marziale's picture "The Circumcision." But his researches on this subject failed to impress the experts, and the picture is now called "Portraits d'hommes" and is still ascribed to Cariani.

In November of 1888 the *Universal Review* published Butler's article on "The Sanctuary of Montrigone." In this article he is still looking for additional works to be identified as Tabachetti's. The lightly bantering tone in which he discusses such questions as mothers-in-law and medieval methods of eating eggs gives the essay an odd charm. It illustrates Butler's conviction that "it is not until faith begins to be weak that it fears an occasional lighter treatment of semi-sacred subjects" (*Collected Essays*, II, 159).

Over a long period Butler had been having a controversy with the authorities of the museum at Basle concerning the authenticity of a drawing there by which he was first struck in 1871, and which he had endeavored to copy in 1884, 1885, and 1886. In his study of this drawing, he became gradually convinced that it was a Holbein original. The museum authorities had listed it as an 1850 copy. On the evidence Butler provided, they listed it as a 1624 copy, but refused to admit it to be by Holbein. After writing a long letter to *The Academy* (October 23, 1886) and after issuing two printed cards of the picture, Butler presented his entire case in an article on "L'Affaire Holbein-Rippel" in the *Universal Review* (November, 1889). The article is an excellent example of the painstaking work Butler could do on such a subject. He must have spent many, many days of research and much energy in pushing his case with experts without seeming to care whether he bored them or not. His arguments seem so convincing we really wonder why they were rejected. But we wonder, too, why Butler felt it incumbent upon him to spend so much time on this controversy. Did he feel that he alone must champion the unrecognized offspring of greatness? Did this drawing of dancing revelers so arouse his pagan spirit that he could not leave it alone?

In the December issue of the *Universal Review* appeared "A Medieval Girl School," in which Butler gives a gently humorous account of the chapels at Oropa. Again he decries the seriousness with which the English take their religion. Again he protests the blindness of tradition which shuts man's eyes to things of value because they have not been recognized by others. ". . . there is no hedge," he says, "so thick or so thorny as the dulness of culture" (*Collected Essays*, II, 204). He evinces a very Victorian desire to have a picture tell a story, and he enjoys figuring out what that story is. He also makes a striking statement of the attitude of scientists and churchmen toward truth:

It seems to me that in the matter of accuracy, priests and men of science whether lay or regular on the one hand, and plain people . . . on the other, are trying to play a different game, and fail to understand one another because they do not see that their objects are not the same. The cleric and the man of science (who is only the cleric in his latest development) are trying to develop a throat with two distinct passages—one that shall refuse to pass even the smallest gnat, and the other that shall gracefully gulp even the largest camel; whereas we men of the street desire but one throat, and are content that this shall swallow nothing bigger than a pony. (*Collected Essays*, II, 210)

And he urges the Church to give up her literal beliefs so that intelligent man may join her.

VII *Science Lectures*

During the year 1882 Butler was twice invited to lecture at the Working Men's College, and he chose memory as his subject. In 1887 he lectured again, this time "On the Genesis of Feeling." In this lecture he views the nervous system as a kind of complex telegraph network evolved by evolutionary processes for the purpose of transmitting feelings which, originating as a sense of shock, had evolved into a complex basis for thought—"feeling being only opinion writ small" (*Collected Essays*, I, 193). He also argues that, just as words are arbitrary names of things, so also are ideas, since they too "have reference to our own convenience rather than to the thing itself" (204). "Will, effort, and deliberation have been essential factors in the formation of the idea from its earliest inception to its most matured form," he says, thus taking his stand with the evolutionary positivists of the nineteenth century. "I make use and disuse," he adds, "the main factor of mental as much as of physical evolution" (206). At the lecture's conclusion he asks: "What is the secret of learning to feel rightly?"

and replies, "To wish to feel more accurately is the first stage.
. . . And the second is like unto it: try to do so." So, he concludes, "Never say that you feel a thing unless you feel it distinctly; and if you do not feel it distinctly, say at once that you
do not as yet quite know your own mind" (209-10).

In March, 1887, Butler lectured on "The Subdivisions of the
Organic World into Animal and Vegetable." This lecture, later
printed in *Science and Art* (May, June, 1887), suggests that the
existence of two main branches of living beings can be traced to
the opposing philosophies (1) of lying in wait for what comes to
one (vegetable) or (2) of going hunting for what one wants
(animal). In addition to developing this thesis, the lecture contains many effective remarks upon the principles to be followed
in formulating any theory—in not pushing too far beyond common sense; in realizing that in the last analysis everything, except
for the frozen thoughts of the inorganic realm, ends in contradiction; and in being aware of the real difficulty of opening up again
a discussion which has been so long settled as to be a part of our
unconscious minds. The essay is excellent; it reveals Butler's
speculative powers at their best.

VIII   *Two Humorous Articles*

In a lighter vein, he wrote two pieces for the *Universal Review*.
In "Quis Desiderio . . . ?" he bewails the disappearance from
the reference shelves of the British Museum of Dr. John Frost's
Lives of Eminent Christians, which for a dozen years he had
used as a writing desk. "It is not the custom of modern writers,"
says Butler, "to refer to the works to which they are most deeply
indebted, . . . but it is to this book alone that I have looked for
support during many years of literary labour, and it is round this
to me invaluable volume that all my own have, page by page,
grown up" (*Collected Essays*, II, 106). Somehow, he gets onto
the subject of Wordsworth's Lucy and speculates that "Wordsworth had murdered her either by cutting her throat or smother-
ing her, in concert, perhaps, with his friends Southey and Cole-
ridge; and, if he had thus found himself released from an engagement which had become irksome to him—or possibly from
the threat of an action for breach of promise—then there is not
a syllable in the poem with which he crowns his crime that is not
alive with meaning" (108). In the second of the two articles,

"The Aunt, the Nieces, and the Dog," he reproduces some old letters he found among his grandfather's papers and some which Jones had lent him, and he revels in their triviality and in their illiterate spelling. He concludes with some Erewhonian remarks about the important function of universities in keeping down the amount of originality in society, the obverse side of his more usual appeal to each of us to see the world with his own eyes. "Our public schools and universities," he says, "play the beneficent part in our social scheme that cattle do in forests: they browse the seedlings down and prevent the growth of all but the luckiest and sturdiest. . . . If a young man, in spite of every effort to fit him with blinkers, will insist on getting rid of them, he must do so at his own risk" (128).

IX *"The Deadlock in Darwinism"*

The April, May, and June, 1890, issues of the *Universal Review* contained three articles by Butler on "The Deadlock in Darwinism." He begins by restating the differences between Lamarckianism and Darwinism, demonstrating once more that Charles Darwin had frequently hedged and had often adopted the use-and-disuse theory. He finds examples of similar hedging in Alfred Russel Wallace, the co-discoverer of the "Survival of the Fittest" theory. The most interesting part of the article is the discussion of August Weismann, the German biologist who had just advanced the claim that germ cells are passed on unchanged from generation to generation. In Weismann, as in Darwin and Wallace, Butler finds ambiguity. Weismann writes that "the assumption that changes induced by external conditions in the organism as a whole are communicated to the germ-cells" may "occasionally" prove correct. Butler calls this letting in the thin edge of the wedge, which is all that Lamarckianism needs (36-37). He says of these writers: "I become like a fly in a windowpane. I see the sunshine and freedom beyond, and buzz up and down their pages, ever hopeful to get through them to the fresh air without, but ever kept back by a mysterious something, which I feel but cannot grasp or see" (39). Is he really saying that, for him, the depersonalized view that science takes is impossible because it annihilates all that makes life livable? In the last of the three articles he restates his *Life and Habit* theory, and he points out that some of the leading biologists have begun to adopt it but that no one has explored its implications. "Why," he asks, "have so many of our leaders shown such a strong hankering after the theory, if there is nothing in it?" (56).

X *"Thought and Language"*

In March, 1890, Butler again lectured at the Working Men's College, this time on "Thought and Language." He attacked Max Müller's contention (*Science of Language,* 1861, and *Three Lectures on the Science of Language,* 1889) that no thought exists without language and that animals are incapable of reason. He gives many examples of the language of gesture and expression and of animal reasoning; then he comments: "After all, a professor, whether of philology, psychology, biology, or any other ology, is hardly the kind of person to whom we should appeal on such an elementary question as that of animal intelligence and language. We might as well ask a botanist to tell us whether grass grows, or a meteorologist to tell us if it has left off raining" (82).[12] Butler realized that his theory of evolution would tolerate no gap between animals and men in ability to communicate and reason, and the idea was abhorrent as well to his own intuitive sympathy with others—for, as he says, if we will not admit that animals can think, why should we believe that other people beside ourselves can either? In addition, the idea went against his recognition of unconscious processes. Describing two fighting pugilists, he says: ". . . the main part of the fighting will be done without any internal concomitance of articulated phrases. Yet we cannot doubt that their action . . . is guided by intelligence and reason . . . reason or thought, for the most part, flies along over the heads of words, working its own mysterious way in paths that are beyond our ken" (86-87).

XI Life of Dr. Samuel Butler

In 1888 the Shrewsbury Archaeological Society asked Butler to prepare a memoir of his grandfather, the Headmaster of Shrewsbury School and Bishop of Lichfield (1774-1839). His sisters sent Butler the bishop's correspondence, and it so intrigued him that he soon decided to write a full-length study rather than the forty to eighty pages the society had requested. As he read the letters entrusted to him, Butler found in his grandfather a person he could heartily admire: his manliness, calm self-possession, scholarliness, and kindliness appealed to him immensely. He was soon more in sympathy with the straightforwardness of the period—having more in it as it did of the eighteenth than of the nineetenth century—than he was with his contemporary world. He was sorry that he had been as hard on George Pontifex in his novel as he had, for he had created this character in accordance with the impression he had of his grandfather at that time. He wished to revise that part of the novel, although he never did so.[13]

The clarity and directness of the style of writing in those days delighted him immensely—it was like his own; and the vigor of the controversies and the trials and tribulations and successes of Dr. Butler gave him a vision of a life he felt he would have loved. His aim in writing the book soon came to be not to pass judgment or to explain but simply to set as much of the material before the reader as he possibly could. He wished to show not only his grandfather as he had lived, but also the school and the church of his time. He packed his book full of letters and copious extracts from all kinds of documents, and it grew to immense size. He later said that writing this book had taught him more than anything else he had ever done.[14] The men of his grandfather's generation, he found, were genuine and honest; they understood the value of common sense and sound judgment; and they were not frightened by inroads of speculation. Though openminded, they possessed a conviction of order and of their own worth that was not shattered by the advent of the imperious scientific spirit. Butler was at home with them. They represented the Towneley spirit, but in a context of sensitivity and scholarliness, service and faith not stultified by false culture and pretense.

During 1889 Butler spent much time gathering material for this biography; he collected additional letters, interviewed dozens of people who remembered his grandfather, and left no stone unturned in his investigations.[15] But his researches took longer than he had anticipated, and five years passed before he finally sent the manuscript to a publisher. He had begun to realize by now that his books might succeed better if he could get them printed at a publisher's risk rather than by underwriting them himself. He engaged a literary agent, and tried his best to find a commercial outlet for the study of his grandfather and for the works on Homer to which we will shortly come. He was unsuccessful, however. *The Life and Letters of Dr. Samuel Butler* was rejected by the Oxford and Cambridge presses, by John Murray, and by others. Finally, Butler cut it by a third and commissioned John Murray to produce it.[16]

The Life and Letters is a leisurely biography, stuffed with characteristic passages revealing the spirit of the late eighteenth and early nineteenth centuries. A storehouse of all sorts of odd information, it makes fascinating reading because of its concreteness. We see all through it that Butler revered and loved his material and his grandfather so much that he did not wish to touch them, but rather longed to see them just as they were. In no other volume does he obtrude himself upon his reader so little as in this. And here may be the greatest obtrusion of all, for we cannot escape the reverential atmosphere. The method he uses is the antithesis of Lytton Strachey's. The book is in a sense a storehouse of history rather than an interpretation. For example, Butler presents a vast supply of facts about the English public-school system, but nowhere does he evaluate or criticize. We might conclude, if we knew nothing else from his pen, that he regarded the system as well-nigh perfect. Had his encounters with the brash presumptuousness of the scientific spirit persuaded him that classical education, like the church, was indeed better than recent developments? A spirit of enlightened and kindly conservatism pervades this little-read biography. It does not forecast the renewed satire of *Erewhon Revisited*.

The critics were at last really pleased with something Butler had done. The *Spectator*[17] regretted that he had reduced the work from twelve hundred to eight hundred pages. *The Athenaeum*[18] gave the book a five-column, front-page review. "We have to thank Mr. Butler," it said, "for a really interesting work —one all the better for being free from the conventional tone of the ordinary biographer. . . . The book is compiled with Mr. Butler's well-known skill." *The Academy*,[19] on the other hand, called the work too long and not interpretative enough. Queen Victoria, however, had her thanks conveyed to Butler and he received many letters of congratulation.[20] For once, he had attacked no prejudices, touched no sore spots. The results were gratifying, but not what his deepest genius continued to require of him. He would not long remain so civilized.

CHAPTER 10

New Heresies

I *Two Discoveries?*

JONES relates that a mention of the *Odyssey* in Canon Ainger's book on Lamb suggested to Butler the idea of an oratorio on Ulysses. His studies for this musical work led him in 1891 to re-read the *Odyssey* in the original.[1] Of this rereading Butler remarks: "The more I reflected on the words, so luminous and so transparent, the more I felt a darkness behind them that I must pierce before I could see the heart of the writer—and this was what I wanted; for art is only interesting in so far as it reveals an artist" (*The Authoress,* 6). With characteristic thoroughness, he set to work to translate the *Odyssey,* searching as he did so for anything that would answer his vague questionings. "It was not till I got to Circe," he tells us, "that it flashed upon me that I was reading the work not of an old man but of a young woman" (8). This intuitive insight having seized him, he gathered all the internal evidence he could to back it up. In addition, he added insult to injury by emulating Heinrich Schliemann. "He made a list of the various natural features of Scheria, as detailed in the poem, and set about looking in the map for some spot that should satisfy all the requirements."[2] This spot he concluded to be Trapani and Mount Eryx in Sicily, and he promptly announced his discovery in two letters to *The Athenaeum.*[3]

Not since his work on *Life and Habit* had anything excited him so much. For the last ten years of his life, he threw himself heart and soul into a defense of these two "discoveries," and he exhausted himself with travel and work in the process. His detached and humorous observation of life almost deserted him at times. He was so far from being a Laodicean or a sideline-sitter that he had to remind himself constantly of the value of the *surtout point de zèle* doctrine to keep control of his enthusiasms. He claimed, of course, that his proposals were tentative and that he awaited refutation by the experts. But by this time he should have known that the experts would greet him with silent contempt as an interloper whose ideas were beneath their consideration. Once again, he was trying to arouse them by presenting a mass of evidence carefully worked up after their own fashion and then by proving that they would not give it a fair chance in court. But this time the silence that greeted Butler came near to breaking his heart.

Not that he did not win some converts. Jones tells us that Lord Grimthorpe, Justice Wills, and George Bernard Shaw were convinced (xxvii); and more recently Robert Graves says, "While working on an explanatory dictionary of Greek myths, I found Butler's arguments for a western Sicilian setting and for a female authorship irrefutable." [4] But this is small success for a project of which Butler himself said, "Nothing has ever interested me (except, of course, Handel) so much as this *Odyssey* business has done; it is far the finest piece of good fortune that ever happened to me, and I find it all the sweeter for the strong displeasure it has aroused in academic circles." [5] The man was incorrigible. He was going to prove that the complacent experts of his "cultured" society were not what they pretended to be, even if it killed him to do so.

His excitement is pathetically revealed in a passage in Jones' biography. "He found scarcely any one in England who took any intelligent interest in the subject. . . . He used, therefore, to talk about the *Odyssey* to me, coming to my rooms evening after evening, inventing the objections which his opponents ought to have raised, considering them, adopting them tentatively, and finally embracing them with such ardour that he crushed them to pieces." When Jones tried to interest him in other subjects, Butler would listen politely, with his mind far away with Nausicaä, and then return to the discussion of the *Odyssey*. "This incessant dwelling upon one subject at last began to produce its effect. . . . [On his way home] he . . . felt giddy and was obliged to hold on to the railings to keep himself from falling." [6]

II   The Authoress of the Odyssey

The main argument of *The Authoress of the Odyssey* is beautifully put together and is sustained by such a wealth of detailed reference to the *Odyssey* and the *Iliad* that it becomes more and more compelling to the reader who follows it with an open mind. Butler was sincere in his contention that he wanted nothing so much as an answer to the reasoning that led him to his convictions. "What can it matter to me where the Odyssey was written, or whether it was written by a man or a woman? From the bottom of my heart I can say truly that I do not care about the way in which these points are decided, but I do care, and very greatly, about knowing which way they are decided by sensible people who have considered what I have urged in this book" (281). The trouble was that the sort of points he urged, as in his books on evolution, were not the sort with which specialists were willing to deal. Perhaps Butler was right to continue his lifelong search for "sensible people," and his tragedy lay in the fact that there are so few of them. Not that they would necessarily have agreed with him. They might, however, have given him the kind of counterdiscussion which would have helped him enrich his own thinking. A few of them did do this in private conversation with him; to them he was grateful.

In *The Authoress,* as in *Unconscious Memory,* Butler gives much attention to the steps in his own thinking that led to his unorthodox conclusions. It is certainly true that for him the "truth" is always such a human thing that it can only be fully realized in terms of the personal, individual insights leading up to it. Butler is not being egotistical but faithful to his own convictions in giving the biography of his speculations, and we wonder if the world of scholarship would be healthier if all scholars could bring themselves to do this. Of course some may say that Butler was unaware of the "real" reasons behind his speculations, as most of us generally are, and that in ascribing the *Odyssey* to a woman he was unconsciously doing penance for his suppression of the desire to have a wife. Yet, if he could have discovered this, supposing it to be true, his work might have been only the richer for the knowledge. However this may be, as he follows the *Odyssey* step by step, discussing detail after detail, we are forced to ask ourselves whether we know the poem nearly as well as he does (he knew large parts of it by heart), and also to ask what counterproposals we can supply to each telling argument he advances. There is much reading into the poem of Butler's own attitudes toward life: toward men and women, and what they are likely to do and not do; toward what is humorous; and toward

the possible ways in which an artist can create his art. If these attitudes are not ours, we tend to reject his deductions. But are
our attitudes more valid? We are in the presence here of the subjective factor in literature which cannot be escaped if literature
is to retain its power to move the individual reader.

The Authoress is indeed a sophisticated version of the sort of
thing students produce when given assignments such as "Write a
character sketch of Captain Ahab." Is no value at all to be derived
from such exercises? Certainly Butler knew his text as no school-
boy would. Are we to say then that his argument is vitiated only
because his point of view differs from ours? Personally, I must
confess that, although I am undecided about his overriding thesis,
I have learned a great deal about the Odyssey from studying his
analysis of it. Butler was certainly justified, from my point of
view, in writing it and in doing the research that led to his writing it. Perhaps we should let the future decide whether this work
of his was a "misdirection of energies." [7] Intuitive ideas so often
turn out to be right, after all, that it is unsafe to decide the issue
dogmatically on the basis of time-bound opposing principles. We
are not so inclined today as the Victorians were to believe that
"art is only interesting in so far as it reveals an artist" [8] or to worry
about the exact geographical details of an ancient poem or about
the sex of its author. Dickens discovered from internal evidence
that George Eliot was a woman, but then he could verify the
truth of his discovery by asking her publisher. Perhaps in the future scholarship will once again become interested in the sort of
issues Butler found so fascinating.

The Saturday Review[9] made a comment on The Authoress
which Butler must have appreciated: "We do not disdain Mr.
Butler's book. It is written with great vivacity, and if it takes a
number of readers to the pure and beautiful text of the 'Odyssey'
and induces them to treat it, not as a dusty school-book, but as a
living and sensitive portion of literature, its action will not have
been in vain." And Notes and Queries[10] gave the book a really favorable review, calling Butler "far too fine and accurate a scholar
to be calmly pooh-poohed." It added, "There are . . . some
editors of Greek texts to whom we may justly look for a response,
seeing that the points raised can no longer be ignored." The response was not forthcoming. But it is good that at least one reviewer saw the issue about which Butler felt so strongly.

III *Translating Homer*

His renewed study of the *Iliad* and the *Odyssey* drew Butler's attention to the fact that there was no English translation of the two poems into simple, straightforward, contemporary prose. "He who would write a translation like those of the Elizabethans," he said, "must above all else avoid Elizabethanisms." [11] His conviction was that "a translation should depart hardly at all from the modes of speech current in the translator's own times" (*The Iliad*, xiii). He wanted to make a translation "with the same benevolent leaning (say) towards Tottenham Court Road that Messrs. Butcher and Lang have shown toward Wardour Street." [12] In his *Note-Books* Butler says: "If you wish to preserve the spirit of a dead author, you must not skin him, stuff him, and set him up in a case. . . . The difference between the Andrew Lang manner of translating the Odyssey and mine is that between making a mummy and a baby. He tries to preserve a corpse . . . whereas I try to originate a new life and one that is instinct (as far as I can effect this) with the spirit though not the form of the original" (197).

This was a noble ambition; and, if Butler's translations suffer for the modern reader from being touched by Victorian colloquialism, perhaps it is only the beginning of "the mosses and lichens which Time will grow" (xiii). The Butler translations are still very readable indeed and have been widely circulated. Though scholars continue to complain about their casual, unpoetic quality, as they do also about that of the Rouse translations which have pushed the Butler method much further than he would have gone, it is notorious that academic people are not usually interested in the enjoyment of literature. The fine Lattimore translation of the *Iliad* in our time is far closer to the spirit of the original and far ahead of Butler's version in beauty, but the beginner will not usually move through it as easily as he will through Butler or Rouse, nor will he be so fully engaged.

The Academy,[13] furious about the new translation, called it "woefully superfluous" and claimed that by discarding archaic expressions Butler had ruined the whole tone of the poem. But *The Athenaeum*[14] cast its vote for "the increased naturalness and simplicity of Butler" and was grateful for the "vivid and direct prose" reminiscent of Hobbes. *Notes and Queries*[15] said: "No student of

Homer more zealous, accomplished and devoted than he can our country boast. . . . We know no English work which will give the average English reader a better insight into Homer." But only 157 copies of the *Iliad* translation were sold in the first year after its publication.[16]

IV *"The Humour of Homer"*

A lecture on "The Humour of Homer," which Butler gave at the Working Men's College in 1892 and later published, still arouses interest in the *Iliad,* just as *The Authoress* does in the *Odyssey.* Butler's lecture is an example of the spirit of paganism and laughter bringing a subject to life. The *Spectator,*[17] of course, was duly shocked: "If Homer were what Mr. Butler represents him to be, he would be, not a great epic poet who commands all the springs of irony, humour, tenderness, and pathos alike, but a proficient in nauseous burlesque and the chaff of the nineteenth-century clubman."

V *Ambiguities in Butler's Life*

Psychologists tell us that men who do not marry and raise a family are forced to project upon their creative work the love they might have felt for their offspring. In this process cruel ambiguities arise; and Butler's life was not devoid of these ambiguities, which to an extent caught up with him during his final years. He had had relations with prostitutes while a student at Cambridge[18] and for twenty years was continually faithful to a mistress, Madame Dumas (who said of Butler "Il sait tout; il ne sait rien; il est poète."[19]) But he was afraid of Miss Savage who, he thought, wanted him to marry her at a time when he could not afford marriage and his literary work.[20] Moreover, a strange emotionalism pervaded his friendship with Charles Paine Pauli.[21] In 1893 Jones introduced Butler to an acquaintance of his, Hans Faesch from Basel, then thirty years old, to whom Butler became very attached. On Hans's departure from London two years later Butler wrote "In Memoriam, H.R.F." (*Note-Books,* 422-23), a poem charged with feeling; and he followed it with letters evincing the strongest affection. The fact probably is that something deep within him longed for a son, as the story of George in *Erewhon Revisited* tends to prove.

VI   Shakespeare's Sonnets Reconsidered

In 1895 Butler began a close study of Shakespeare's *Sonnets*, for he believed that internal evidence might unlock their secret, just as he was confident it had unlocked for him that of the *Odyssey*. The results he achieved, however, have some of the characteristics of a projective test, since he was dealing in the emotional lyricism of these great poems with materials which could hardly be made objective.

Shakespeare's Sonnets Reconsidered and in Part Rearranged was published in 1899. It is probably the first full-scale assault on the apparently insoluble problem of the story behind these poems. There had been much speculation about the identity of Mr. W. H.; about the dating of the poems; and about individual passages, which Butler brilliantly summarizes and discusses. But no one had ever had the audacity to go through the sonnets detail by detail and to pretend that he could fit them together into a coherent whole. The Victorians were embarrassed by the sonnets and apologetic, as is well exemplified in Edward Dowden's gingerly discussion.[22] They preferred to steer clear of the sort of conclusion that Butler drew, in comparing the sonnets with the *Iliad*: "Whereas the love of Achilles for Patroclus depicted by the Greek poet is purely English, absolutely without taint or alloy of any kind, the love of the English poet for Mr. W. H. was, though only for a short time, more Greek than English" (145).

Part of Butler's argument, though, turns on a puzzlingly literal interpretation of Sonnet 33. He deduces from the preceding sonnets that Mr. W. H. "in concert with others" laid a trap for the poet, and that he was "made to 'travel forth without' that 'cloak' which, if he had not been lured, we may be sure that he would not have discarded. Hardly had he laid the cloak aside before he was surprised according to a preconcerted scheme, and very probably roughly handled, for we find him lame soon afterwards . . . and apparently not fully recovered a twelvemonth later" (82-83). Butler is certain that the sonnets must be very early works because they thus record the indiscretions of youth, which could not be forgiven an older man. He argues that Sonnet 107 refers to the defeat of the Spanish Armada, and from this he deduces that the poems belong to the years 1585-1588.

How, we wonder, could Butler feel so confident of the unlikely story he *makes* these poems tell? This book, like his other literary detective work, shows evidence of much careful labor, and it explores with skill the defective arguments of many previous scholars. But, having memorized the whole sonnet sequence, having meditated on it for months, and having examined in the British Museum most of the scholarship on the subject, Butler draws from it a story built on a chain of such tenuous inferences and doubtful interpretations that the reader gasps with amazement. Of course, however, if we were challenged to do better, we admit in all candor that we could not.[23]

Perhaps the difference between us and Butler is that we are content to enjoy each poem for what it is without feeling his driving compulsion to get to a story beneath. We may even be convinced that there never was a story at all. Butler has this to say to us: "It may be asked, Why have a story, when the one which Q alone permits is throughout painful and in parts repulsive? Many, indeed, say 'Read the Sonnets if you like, but do not go below their surface; let their music and beauty of expression be enough.' I do not write for these good people, nor are they likely to read me; I therefore pass them by at as wide a distance as I can" (100). After being thus shoved aside, we may admit that we too should like to understand the story; but we should then add that we cannot accept the interpretation Butler provides. We would finally acknowledge, however, that his book has done us a service as did his book on the *Odyssey*. It has made us think about the sonnets more carefully than we ever had before, and perhaps that was all that Butler really wanted. We would then agree with *The Academy*[24] that it is a work which "no serious student can afford to neglect," and with *Notes and Queries*[25] that "all that Mr. Butler says is scholarly, ingenious and worthy of attention." But still we wonder why he pushed so fast and went so far. Was he desperate for one great discovery before he died that would be his acknowledged child—the world having cruelly cast aside all he had so far laid on the altar of immortality?

CHAPTER 11

Alpha and Omega

I   Erewhon Revisited

SINCE 1872 the ideas of *Erewhon* and plans for *Erewhon Revisited* had never been far from Butler's mind. His notes show a gradual accumulation of suggestions to be added to the *Erewhon* material. In 1896 he told Mr. Fisher Unwin that he had often thought of writing a sequel to his early book, and in 1900 he began work on it.[1] When, in the spring of 1901, Longmans declined to publish the newly completed volume because it would give offense "to his connection among the High Anglican party," [2] Butler wrote to George Bernard Shaw, who had praised the *Odyssey* theory when Butler addressed the Fabian Society ("not, heaven forbid, that I belong to or have any sympathy with the Fabian Society" [3]). He asked Shaw what publisher he would recommend, and Shaw promptly persuaded Grant Richards to undertake the book and also to publish a revised edition of *Erewhon*. Thus Richards became the first publisher to assume a financial risk for a book by Butler.[4]

Erewhon Revisited is narrated by the son of Arowhena and Higgs, born after their arrival in England, who reports to us the story his father tells just before his death. According to this story, Higgs returns to Erewhon thirty years after his escape, via the same route he had previously taken. He is motivated to take the journey in part by the desire to get there before Chowbok, his former guide, who is planning a trip of conquest. On his arrival, Higgs discovers that the Erewhonians have founded a religion based upon his previous brief sojourn in the country. He discovers that a son of his, George, was born to Yram, the jailkeeper's daughter, and that the authorities who interpret his doctrine and head the new religion of Sunchildism are so well entrenched that they will not tolerate his return but will destroy him rather than give up their magic. With some difficulty he disguises himself, though Yram and George soon guess who he is. Wandering around the countryside, he observes the changes which have taken place in the customs of the country since his previous visit and is not pleased to find that many Erewhonian beliefs seem more fatuous and extreme than ever.

The plot centers on the dedication ceremonies of a new cathedral erected in honor of Higgs. George is so appalled by the hokus-pokus of the established religion that, before he recognizes Higgs, he states his wish that the Sunchild (Higgs) might return and vindicate himself by renouncing the nonsense that has been created in his name. This Higgs does at a dramatic moment during the dedication ceremony, thus winning his son's respect (though it turns out that few believe his statement). He then flees for his life, but not until after he has given the leaders of the church some sound advice regarding the necessity for moderation in things divine. Soon after his hurried return to England, Higgs dies, and his son, the narrator, journeys to Erewhon to deliver to George his part of the inheritance.

For the modern reader, *Erewhon Revisited* is somewhat marred by a too-exciting and too-ingenious plot. Once more Butler tried hard to write a book that would be a success, and he weakened his tale by the overuse of suspense in the manner of a writer of fiction for children. The improbabilities and excitement seem manufactured by a force alien to anything Butler had previously given in to. There is a touch of the fake good fellowship and joviality of Tom Swift in many passages.[5] Nevertheless, this quality does not hide the book's genuine merits. *Erewhon Revisited* has an obvious unity, which *Erewhon* never had. The characters are believable and, some of them, very amusing. The central theme is well sustained. The book has won a warm place in the hearts of many readers, some of whom value it even more highly than *Erewhon* itself.

II *The New Religion*

Butler asked himself what evolutionary changes would have occurred in the land of Erewhon since the departure of his hero thirty years before. He concluded that the Erewhonians would have developed a new religion based upon "the apparently miraculous ascent of a remarkable stranger into the heavens with an earthly bride" (*Erewhon Revisited*, xxiii), but he warned his readers that he had no specific analogy with any real religion in mind. He envisioned his hero, like himself, as having passed through a crisis on his return to England "through his own want of tact, and a highly-strung nervous state, which led him to attach too much importance to his own discoveries, and not enough to those of other people" (2). Erewhon had remained unexplored because those who went there never returned—they were drowned in an ominous blue pool—and also because there was no gold in the mountain range. Is Butler warning others of the dangers of the inverted kingdoms he had spent his life exploring and of the lack of reward for such exploration?

Chowbok, a kind of Darwin of this romance, circulates rumors that Higgs is an alcoholic and thus discredits him. Fortunately, though, Higgs inherits wealth; and, in 1890, he cannot resist his burning desire to revisit the strange kingdom of his earlier adventures. On his second return to England, much sooner than expected, he is "an altered man." He barely manages to tell his story to his son John, who narrates it to us, before his mind snaps completely and he dies. "Remember," he says, "that I thought I was quite well as long as I was in Erewhon" (13); but he is obviously far from well in England. Can no one else exist in both these realms at once as Butler succeeded in doing?

His son tells us that his father's second trip to Erewhon was much easier than the first trip had been. "Was he being lured on to his destruction by some malicious fiend, or befriended by one who had compassion on him and wished him well?" (18). "The intervening twenty years—most of them grim ones—rose up mockingly before him, and the buoyancy of hope yielded to the despondency of admitted failure" (17). On ascending to the top of the pass, Higgs finds the statues—the Ten Commandments—smaller than he had expected, but "not less mysteriously impressive than at first" (20). But once he has passed over the range, surprise after surprise assails him.

Unrecognized, he meets Hanky and Panky (Hokus and Pokus), the academic leaders of the kingdom; both are dressed in garb modeled on the clothes Higgs had worn on his previous visit, though Panky wears his reversed. Hanky, Professor of Worldly Wisdom at Bridgeford, the city of the people who are above suspicion, gets Higgs' gold from him by assuring him that it is not gold (the *Life and Habit* theory?), though Higgs soon after steals it back again. Higgs discovers that Hanky burned the clothes he left in Erewhon when they were entrusted to him for study, and that Hanky had even tried to burn Yram along with them, like the experts who destroy the evidence in an argument.[6] Panky, the old ritualist, busies himself emending texts. When Higgs says, "Forgive us our trespasses as we forgive them that trespass against us," Panky points out the absurdity of this. ". . . the correct reading," he says, "should obviously be 'Forgive us our trespasses but do not forgive them that trespass against us.' This makes sense, and turns an impossible prayer into one that goes straight to the heart of every one of us" (41).

The fun continues and becomes more complex as the story progresses. Hanky is a hard-boiled realist. He knows full well and admits in private discussion that Sunchildism is a hoax from beginning to end, but he is perfectly willing to run it for his own advantage. He is a Jesuit; for, although he is a hypocrite, he does not deceive himself. Butler has a certain realistic respect for him. Panky, on the other hand, cannot frankly admit the truth; "he had thrown himself so earnestly into his work that he had become a living lie" (31). In England he would have been a High Church ritualist. Dr. Downie, another Erewhonian theologian, is a hopeful figure. He will neither preach nor write against Sunchildism, but will live lukewarmly against it; and this attitude is what the Hankeys and Pankeys hate.

III *Father and Son*

There is undisguised emotion in Butler's account of the relations between Higgs and his son George. As noted above, George declares to his father, whom he does not yet recognize, that, if the Sunchild would return and publicly announce that he was not divine, he would forgive him and accept him as his father. Would Butler have loved his own father if he had had the courage to tell the truth about what he really believed? The events of the story are arranged to give Higgs a chance to make this admission, and he thus wins for himself the devotion of a son. No critic, so far as I have noted, has recognized in this episode Butler's longing for an honest father; but it is as clearly implied as his longing for a son appears to be.

In this dual relationship lies the deepest theme of the story. It has the quality of some of Butler's poetry—warm, strong, and full of feeling. As a matter of fact there is strong feeling in all of Butler's work, though his clever wit, self-mockery, and bravado seem to hide it from the casual reader. In this idea of a returning divinity who would renounce the false trappings with which an organized church has clothed him is adumbrated the "Grand Inquisitor" theme Dostoevsky developed in *The Brothers Karamazov.* If "Higgs himself were to return," says Higgs to his son, ". . . he would be killed but not believed" (53). "If he [Christ] were to apply for a divorce [from the Church] on the grounds of cruelty, adultery, and desertion," says Butler in his *Note-Books,* "he would probably get one." [7]

Butler expresses his admiration not only for the honest George. He also loves and respects George's resourceful and clever mother Yram, who is the woman Butler might have married had he found her in Victorian England. With feminine tact and intuition, she sees through fraud and insincerity and gets right to the heart of each problem that faces her. She holds the complete love and affection of her husband the mayor, even though he knows that George is not his son. Naturally, she terrifies the two frauds Hanky and Panky as Butler would have liked to terrify the Darwins, Jowetts, Sidney Lees, and Garnetts of his day but never succeeded in doing. She is a more successful Butler, suggesting that his own particular genius had much of the feminine in it.

IV *Compromise and Breakdown*

The denouement of *Erewhon Revisited* has puzzled some readers; for, after his skillful exposure of the frauds of a religion based on misrepresentation, superstition, and power politics, Butler adopts a most pacifistic and compromising tone. Instead of calling for immediate revolt against this monster of hypocrisy, he examines its merits calmly and realistically, and considers the danger that something worse might take over if this religion were suddenly swept aside. And, through his mouthpiece Higgs, who has been schooled by adversity and is no longer the prig he was twenty years before, Butler recommends compromise and only gradual change. "Make me a peg on which to hang all your own best ethical and spiritual conceptions," says Higgs to the professors (220). Such things as the ridiculous worship of the droppings from the four horses which are believed to have pulled the balloon aloft—they are miraculously preserved and kept in a golden reliquary—are not to be denied but quietly pushed into the background, and slowly a Broad Church attitude will come to prevail. Not without a struggle does the unheroic decision to take this line come to Higgs. Reason tells him that he should hew to the truth, but instinct advocates compromise. "This was the strongest internal conflict that I ever remember to have felt, and it was at the end of it that I perceived the first, but as yet faint symptoms of that sickness from which I shall not recover" (66). What clearer diagnosis do we need of Butler's own dilemma— whether to serve the cultured, conscious dictates of his age, or the instinctive voice of the unconscious within him, even though it threatened sickness and disaster? Butler himself bravely faced this dilemma and achieved considerable happiness in its despite. "The giddiness," our narrator tells us, speaking of Higgs, "which had for some seconds compelled him to lay hold of the first thing he could catch at in order to avoid falling, passed away" (66-67).

In his advice to Hanky, Panky, and Dr. Downie, Higgs says: "Better a corrupt church than none at all. . . . Those who in my country would step into the church's shoes are as corrupt as the church, and more exacting. They are also more dangerous, for the masses distrust the church, and are on their guard against aggression, whereas they do not suspect the doctrinaires and faddists, who, if they could, would interfere in every concern of our lives. . . . What I have said is nine-tenths of it rotten and wrong, but it is the most practicable rotten and wrong that I can suggest, seeing into what a rotten and wrong state of things you have drifted" (221). What a comment this is on the world Butler lived in, and on the world in which we still live!

Since it stays closer to its central point, *Erewhon Revisited* is not the variegated performance that *Erewhon* was. But it has its fantastic aspects, such as "Mrs. Tantrums, Nagger, certified by the College of Spiritual Athletics. Terms for ordinary nagging, two shillings and sixpence per hour. Hysterics extra" (62). Moreover, there are the requirement for professors at Bridgeford that butter not melt in their mouths and the deformatories where children are taught to lie to prepare them to lead useful lives.

V *Revisions of* Erewhon

In the revision of *Erewhon* which Butler made at this time to secure a renewed copyright there are many brilliant touches which make it the complex book it is. He added the notion that Erewhonians are subjected to punishment for misfortune, especially in money matters (Chapter X); the examples of Europeans who equate crime with disgrace; the subterfuges by which the Erewhonians pretend to have committed a crime to cover up an illness; and the account of the rigorous training straighteners must undergo. To Chapter XI, "Some Erewhonian Trials," he added the trial of a man who was unlucky enough to have lost his wife—"Luck," says the judge, "is the only fit object of human veneration"; and in the next chapter he placed several long discussions of luck. Practically all of Chapter XIII on the Erewhonian view of death is new. In the chapter on the Musical Banks (XV) a long passage on the relation between religion and the "unconscious instinctive wisdom of millions of past generations" is new, as is the passage on divinity at the end of Chapter XVI. Most of Chapter XXII, "The Colleges of Unreason," is also new, including the professor who says "It is not our business to help students to think for themselves," and the discussion of examinations. To "The Book of the Machines" Butler added the discussion of horsepower and of the origin of our admiration for wealth. Chapters XXVI and XXVII on the rights of animals are entirely new, with their fascinating story, full of multiple meanings, of the student who surreptitiously ate meat, found himself healthier and happier, but was so conscience-stricken that he hanged himself. These changes are considerable enough to place within this early work echoes of Butler's thinking throughout his entire life; but—as we noted earlier—it is well to remember that the echoes were not there in 1872.

VI The Note-Books

When Butler was in Canada in 1874 he first began systematically collecting the notes he customarily jotted down each day as thoughts came into his mind which he wished to preserve.[8] As his collection grew, he edited the notes, weeded them out, prepared a definitive index, and entered them in large books of about two hundred and twenty-five pages each. He compiled in this way six complete volumes by the time of his death, and he had enough additional, unedited material to fill two more. He soon discovered that he hardly ever used these notes, but he realized that writing them helped to clear his mind and to fix his ideas in his memory, so he generally devoted the first hour of each day's work to them. In compiling them Butler was actually creating a work of art, though he certainly did not think of the matter this way at the time. When extracts from them were published posthumously in 1912, the response was enthusiastic. They were recognized as an important addition to English literature. As much as any single book that he wrote, they bring before us the lucidity of his mind; his uncanny power of expression; and his kindly, quizzical, original way of viewing life; himself; and all his theories. They are a real testimony to the orderliness and constancy of their author's mind and to his abiding devotion to his work.[9]

Such devotion to passing scraps of thought, whims of a moment, trivialities even, may seem narcissistic; but for Butler it was not this at all. Rejecting so much of the institutionalized philosophy, science, and culture of his day, he was thrown upon his own intuitive perceptions for his raw material, and this he believed was the kind of material with which everyone should work. He regarded the dictates of the individual mind as nearly divine—what did not come from this source was most likely sham and affectation. He was like Thoreau and Emerson in his respect for the insights of his own individual moments. The notes have a tremendous range, from passing thoughts on events of the day to profound philosophical meditations. Their dominant characteristic is the way in which, like his books, they challenge all accepted views, turn traditional patterns upside down, scare, shock, and amuse. What a disciplining in the unusual Butler gave himself in composing them! But we might also ask if they were therapeutic —written daily to clarify these strange perceptions so that he could converse understandably with his fellow man.

The notes cannot be adequately abstracted, summarized, or commented upon. They must be read by anyone who cares to cross his intellect with something different, with thoughts his "mother did not teach [him] at all, nor [his] father . . . but altogether otherwise." Sometimes they provide interesting extensions of Butler's published volumes and suggest lines of speculation he might have followed had he lived longer. Some readers hurry through the notebooks looking for humor, as though they were reading a collection of jokes. This is a mistake. Much thought is embedded in the whimsical, probing fragments of Butler's mind. They are counsels of maturity, courage, and independence. A few characteristic samples from Volume I of the manuscript notebooks are the following: "American Dishonesty—Refer it to their Puritan ancestry." "Ultimate Triumph of Good—When we say that we believe in this, we mean that we are cocksure of our own opinions." "God as now generally conceived of is only the last witch." "Truth on any subject is the opinion which either has, or may come to have the whip-hand." "Someone said of another that he was cultured. 'Yes,' was the rejoinder, 'not to say manured.'" "There is no such metaphysics as physics in the hands of a scientist who goes too far for his facts." "Reason—if you follow it far enough, it always leads to conclusions that are contrary to reason."

In his preface to his second manuscript volume Butler wrote: "It seems to me that [an author] is the worst person . . . to make selections from his own notes, or indeed even, in my case, to write them. I cannot help it. They grew as, with little disturbance, they now stand; they are not meant for publication; the bad ones serve as bread for the jam of the good ones." Yet he adds, "That [the notebooks] will be looked over by not a few I doubt not," and this suggests his awareness that he was writing for more than just himself.

VII *The Jones' Edition*

When Henry Festing Jones undertook the task of preparing the first collection of extracts,[10] he invented a series of headings under which to collect the entries he wished to use; moreover, he did much editing to make the notes fit smoothly together. Thus his volume begins with the topic: "Lord, What is Man?," under which he enters some of Butler's comments on mankind, among them the following: "A man is a passing mood coming and going in the mind of his country; he is the twitching of a nerve, a smile, a frown, a thought of shame or honour, as it may happen" (1). "A sense of humour keen enough to show a man his own absurdities, as well as those of other people, will keep him from the commission of all sins, or nearly all, save those that are worth committing" (3). "The world may not be particularly wise—still, we know of nothing wiser" (4). "We had better live in others as much as we can if only because we thus live more in the race, which God really does seem to care about a good deal, and less in the individual, to whom, so far as I can see, he is indifferent" (7). "Is life worth living? This is a question for an embryo, not for a man" (9).

The next heading Jones selects is "Elementary Morality." This section begins with the note: "The foundations of morality. These are like other foundations; if you dig too much about them the superstructure will come tumbling down" (17). A long note on the necessity of serving both God and Mammon is included, put together by Jones from a whole series of Butler's entries in various volumes (17-18). There are many examples in this section of Butlerian needling, as for example: "It is the function of vice to keep virtue within reasonable bounds" (21). "Morality turns on whether the pleasure precedes or follows the pain. Thus, it is immoral to get drunk because the headache comes after the drinking, but if the headache came first, and the drunkenness afterwards, it would be moral to get drunk" (22). "To love God is to have good health, good looks, good sense, experience, a kindly nature, and a fair balance of cash in hand" (26). "Heaven is the work of the best and kindest men and women. Hell is the work of prigs, pedants, and professional truth-tellers. The world is an attempt to make the best of both" (28).

The next sections in Jones' volume bring together notes and other materials Butler collected in connection with his books: material for *Erewhon* and for a projected continuation of *Life and Habit,* and material under headings like "Memory and Design," "Vibrations," and "Mind and Matter." A section on "Music, Pictures, and Books" brings together many of his most telling ideas about expression and art. "Thought pure and simple," he writes, "is as near to God as we can get. . . . All the most essential and thinking part of thought is done without words or consciousness. It is not till doubt and consciousness enter that words become possible" (89). "In art," he says, "never try to find out anything, or try to learn anything until the not knowing it has come to be a nuisance to you for some time" (101). "Do not hunt for subjects, let them choose you, not you them" (102). "My books. I never make them; they grow; they come to me and insist on being written, and on being such and such" (102). "If a person is in doubt about this or that in his writing, it will often guide him if he asks himself how it will tell a hundred years hence" (106).

A section on "Handel and Music" follows. Here Butler makes explicit many of his reasons for loving Handel and for disliking Beethoven and Mozart. "A Painter's Views on Painting" develops his ideas on the art which he had tried so hard to make his profession. He explores the value of the apprentice system and the dangers of academicism. "Art," he says, "is at best a dress, important, yet still nothing in comparison with the wearer, and, as a general rule, the less it attracts attention the better" (135). "He is a great artist who can be depended upon not to bark at nothing" (135).

The notes collected under the heading *"Homo Unius Libri"* provide many insights into Butler's attitude toward his own career and reveal the abiding good humor and objectivity which persisted in him in spite of his apparent failures. "He who would propagate an opinion," he says, no doubt thinking of himself, "must begin by making sure of his ground and holding it firmly. There is as little use in trying to breed from weak opinion as from other weak stock, animal or vegetable" (163).

Other headings Jones uses are "Cash and Credit," "Unprofessional Sermons," "Higgledy-Piggledy," and "Written Sketches." In the sketches we see Butler's novelist eye at work, gleaning all sorts of odd scraps of conversation and incident from his daily life which reveal the peculiarities of human nature. "How holy people look when they are sea-sick!" he writes. "There was a patient Parsee near me [on a channel passage] who seemed purified once and for ever from all taint of the flesh. Buddha was a low, worldly-minded, music-hall comic singer in comparison. . . ." (257).

The section Jones puts together on "Truth and Convenience" is a compendium of Butler's pragmatic thinking. "There is no such source of error," he writes, "as the pursuit of absolute truth" (302). "There is no permanent absolute unchangeable truth; what we should pursue is the most convenient arrangement of our ideas" (302). "Truth . . . should be played pretty low down––to the pit and gallery rather than the stalls. Pit-truth is more true to the stalls than stall-truth to the pit" (303). "An essential contradiction in terms meets us at the end of every enquiry" (303). In another section on "First Principles" Butler tells us that "We are not won by arguments that we can analyze, but by tone and temper, by the manner which is the man himself" (335). "It is said," he also comments, that "we can build no superstructure without a foundation of unshakable principles. There are no such principles" (336).

A section on "Rebelliousness" contains some of Butler's notes on God and religion. He says: "If I were to start as a god or a prophet, I think I should take the line: 'Thou shalt not believe in me. Thou shalt not have me for a god. Thou shalt worship any damned thing thou likest except me'" (340). "As an instrument of warfare against vice," he writes, "or as a tool for making virtue, Christianity is a mere flint implement. Christianity is a woman's religion, invented by women and womanish men for themselves" (341). Sections on "Reconciliation," "Death," and "The Life of the World to Come" follow. Finally, Jones concludes his edition of the notebooks with Butler's poetry, including the sonnets and the words to the cantatas "Narcissus" and "Ulysses."

CHAPTER 12

Summation

I *Butler's Influence*

THE story of Butler which remains to be told is the story of the posthumous fame which came to him, as he predicted that it would. When he died in 1902, the obituaries that appeared were kind and considerate but not enthusiastic. R. A. Streatfeild, Butler's literary executor, began the campaign to get him a wider hearing which was carried on during the next decade by Butler's closest friends. An article by Streatfeild in *The Monthly Review*[1] described Butler's life and work in general terms. *The Way of All Flesh,* published in 1903, at first caused little excitement; among the leading journals few reviewed it at length, and *The Athenaeum*[2] described it as a failure. But in 1904 Arnold Bennett read it "with a real zest" and noted that "there is a vast amount of naked truth in the book."[3] Desmond MacCarthy, in an article entitled "The Author of Erewhon,"[4] was the first to point out that all of Butler's works illustrate a general philosophy of life. He called Butler "a frank and consistent hedonist."

In 1907 Streatfeild began in *The New Quarterly Review* a series of extracts from *The Note-Books* (1907-1910), and in 1908 several of Butler's books were reissued. The annual *Erewhon* dinners, begun in 1908 by Marcus Hartog and Henry Festing Jones, continued until the outbreak of World War I. Among the speakers at these dinners were George Bernard Shaw, Edmund Gosse, Gilbert Cannan, Angus Birrell, and Desmond MacCarthy. Clutton-Brock's article in the London *Times Literary Supplement*[5] was a discussion of Butler which drew wide attention. In 1910 W. Bateson, professor of biology at Cambridge, called Butler "the most brilliant, and by far the most interesting of Darwin's opponents" in a volume of essays commemorating the centenary of Darwin's birth.[6] In his *An Introduction to Biology and Other Papers*[7] A. D. Darbishire of the University of Edinburgh made wide use of Butler's biological theories and acknowledged his indebtedness. Another group of writers at this time began to take Butler seriously as a philosopher: Robert F. Rattray in *Mind* [8]; William Barry in *The Dublin Review*[9]; Gerold Pestalozzi in a German dissertation;[10] and May Sinclair in her *A Defence of Idealism.*[11]

George Bernard Shaw's complimentary references to Butler in the prefaces to *Major Barbara* (1907) and *Back to Methuselah* (1921) and the favorable reviews of *The Note-Books* when they appeared in book form in 1912 (the London *Times Literary Supplement* gave it front-page treatment) mark the high point of Butler's early reputation. This period culminated in such remarks as that by Orlo Williams that Butler "is one of the few" of the writers immediately following the great Victorians "whose name is little likely to be forgotten by the generations to come," [12] and that *The Way of All Flesh* "stands with the greatest English novels of the last century." [13]

Gilbert Cannan's book-length study of Butler, published in 1915, is a document of passionate though one-sided hero-worship; Shaw, in reviewing it, took Cannan to task for overlooking Butler's real genius.[14] This book was followed the next year by John F. Harris' quieter but sounder study.[15] W. T. Young, writing on Butler in the 1916 edition of *The Cambridge History of English Literature,*[16] says that although Butler has not "the highest gifts of poetry or emotion . . . he is very far from being a mere indiscriminating wit; he has, in the end, a constructive intention, not mockery, but the liberation of the spirit." [17] In the meantime, many American periodicals and books contained favorable comment on Butler and explored his ideas: Clara Stillman in *The North American Review,*[18] Horace Bridges in *As I Was Saying,*[19] and S. P. B. Mais in *From Shakespeare to O. Henry,*[20] are examples.

Some recent critics suggest that the 1919 publication of Henry Festing Jones' two-volume *Memoir*[21] did Butler a disservice by overwhelming him with petty detail and creating the image of a man who lived a trivial life; but if the effect is trivial, this results more from Jones' rather unimaginative selection of material than from the realities of Butler's own existence, as Mrs. Charles Gogin, who had known Butler well, recognized on reading the book.[22] The work contains an impressive collection of facts which have been used by all later writers on Butler, even those who see him very differently from the way Jones saw him; and only the unwary reader is trapped into accepting Jones' portrait at face value. To an extent, Shaw himself fell into the trap. Reviewing the *Memoir* in the *Manchester Guardian*,[23] he modified his former praise of Butler and described his later years as petty and ridiculous.

If Butler was admired at first for his iconoclastic onslaught on Victorian complacency, his popularity was bound to fade when it became no longer the custom to downgrade the Victorians. But after a period of reassessment which took place in the 1920's, sounder reasons for praising him began to emerge. His works were widely translated and discussed in France and Germany, and critics there readily saw their unity. In the United States, Paul Elmer More inaugurated a more careful study of Butler in *The Unpartizan Review*,[24] finding a deep vein of poetry in Butler which he felt was unfortunately much overlaid, and praising him for a "superbly clear and idiomatic English style." C. E. M. Joad's *Samuel Butler*[25] takes Butler's biological theories very seriously indeed and defends them well, and Louis and Madeleine Cazamian devoted careful attention to him in their works.[26] M. P. Willcocks in *Between the Old World and the New*[27] says that "at bottom, Butler is a man of prodigious faith, as well as of reverence."

It is hard to find any trend in the very considerable amount of Butler criticism that appeared during the 1920's and that has continued to appear ever since. Clara Stillman's *Samuel Butler, a Mid-Victorian Modern*[28] is primarily a study of Butler's ideas but does him an injustice by continually emphasizing his modernity, as though he were chiefly a spokesman for the age to come. This thesis is countered by Sylvia Clark Wilson's findings in a Radcliffe College thesis (1932) that Butler was very much a part of his period, and that all of his major ideas were shared by other Victorians. Robert F. Rattray's *Samuel Butler: A Chronicle and an Introduction*[29] is a serious attempt to set Butler in his entirety before the reader. "The records of Butler," he says, "reveal a heart hungry to love and to be loved." In 1935 Herbert Davis remarked in an article on Butler in the *University of Toronto Quarterly*[30] that unfortunately Butler's reputation is still based on his excursions into literature and not upon the results of his "patient pursuit of knowledge." In 1936 in Malcolm Muggeridge's *A Study of Samuel Butler, the Earnest Atheist* [31] the high point of adverse Butler criticism was reached: as Furbank points out,[32] this work creates a fictional figure based on some of the facts of Butler's life and on the foolish idolatry he aroused in certain quarters, and then savagely destroys this fiction, leaving the real Butler relatively untouched. In 1939 Ernest A. Baker, in his *The History of the English Novel, Vol. X*,[33] called *The Way of All Flesh* "a very great novel" and said that it had had as potent an influence on the modern novel as that exercised by Flaubert, the Goncourts, de Maupassant, and Zola.

The most important recent books on Butler are those by P. N. Furbank[34] and Philip Henderson;[35] these books make use of sharp analysis and precise psychological deductions, but they are in a sense too formalistic, too meticulous. Although both writers claim that Butler was a genius, that fact hardly emerges from their studies. The question suggests itself: Is our present era so exacting in its requirements that the unspecialized, broad, jovial spirit of Samuel Butler must slip through its fingers and be gone? Countering these somewhat negative studies, however, has been a series of more careful scholarly analyses in academic publications which are a straw in the wind of changing fortunes.[36] Who can speculate what the future may hold?

II *Last Word*

Although I am aware that critical opinion has been much divided about Butler's accomplishments, I would list the following as probably his major achievements. He understood and worked with the concept of the unconscious long before Freud, and he made creative use of it in *Life and Habit* and in *The Way of All Flesh*. He grappled with the threat posed by science and the machine in *Erewhon*, when atomic bombs were still unheard of. He subjected the theory of evolution to a searching metaphysical analysis not yet surpassed. He achieved a pragmatic view of truth before William James and John Dewey, and he applied it with stunning effect to religion and morality in *The Fair Haven* and in his notebooks. He wrote a novel, *The Way of All Flesh*, which, after its publication in 1903, became tremendously influential and had an effect on scores of literary men, including such important writers as George Bernard Shaw, Arnold Bennett,

H. G. Wells, and Somerset Maugham. And, above all, he championed simplicity and naturalness and a kind of hearty realism in an era threatened by a top-heavy culture and addicted to a fancy style.

Obviously, then, Butler's books are not, as some have suggested, the products of a neurotic, solipsistic crank who deluded himself into the conviction that they had value. His best passages shock us to a sudden reappraisal of our way of viewing life. They clear the air for us as they did for him. What he accomplished was to apply to the assumptions of his age—and to those of most people of any age—a kind of classical perspicuity of thought, constantly needling his readers to do likewise. He was not so much interested in the specific issues which he attacked as in the methods of attack he used and in his assertion of the right to attack. There is thus a pragmatic ambiguity throughout his work as to what he "really" believed and what he was advancing for the sake of exploring possibilities. He unfailingly challenges us to be equally open about our own beliefs.

He fought with all kinds of experts, not so much because he was sure he was right as because he valued the drama of controversy and wanted to show the world that professionals lack the willingness to defend their findings honestly and logically. His great desire was to cut through the arbitrary, pleasure-robbing fixations of humanity to show men how to become free to be themselves. He was a kind of archindividualist, an anarchist of the mind, although in political outlook he was most conservative.

In spite of his originality, however, Butler was a Victorian, and it is misleading to call him a twentieth-century modern.[37] Rooted in the traditions of his age, he reacted strongly for or against but always in terms of them. He shared with his contemporaries the conviction that all thought must constitute a whole; that the writer must grapple with the nature of truth, science, religion; that academicism and the higher reaches of speculation are suspect; and that literature should be chiefly a device for informing and instructing.[38] He actually prided himself, as a mark of his independence of judgment, on owning few books and on reading few, apart from his studies in the British Museum. He prided himself too on his individuality of taste. The fact that everyone else liked something was often reason enough for him to reject it. But he was highly sensitive to the world around him, and really more a part of it than he cared to admit. The fun of his *Note-Books* is partly lost on readers who do not know the soil from which it sprang; they may find dull what is witty and effective in terms of its occasion. Butler pushed at the boundaries of Victorianism, as did so many leaders of his day.[39] He is one of the liveliest examples of the Victorian advance. Rejected by his contemporaries because he probed too sharply and too hard and demanded too much of them, he was not so completely rejected as many have thought he was.[40]

III *L'envoi*

This study has concerned itself with some of the work of a man haunted by strange and rebellious insights, who avoided the clichés of criticism and thus deserves not to have them applied to him. Butler worshiped Handel above all other men because he found in his music the serene self-command he himself strove for and came as near to finding as the creative spirit generally can. And he feared Beethoven and other great masters, though not Shakespeare or Homer, because he could not trust himself to the Dionysian possibilities they suggested. In a way, they were too like himself. He had an intense, impassioned love for honesty and clarity of thought which made him assail the intellectual confusions of his age, though he may sometimes have been guilty of creating new confusions of his own. But combined with this he possessed an uncannily modern awareness of the limitations of logic and of the mind. He fought against a science and an academicism which in our day have conquered the earth and built an atom bomb, making the terms of his battle of renewed importance to us. He stood firmly for the right of the amateur to criticize and evaluate the work of specialists—a right without which a democracy like our own cannot hope to survive.

Was Butler a great creative artist? If the categories of our own form-conscious age are applied to his variegated and often odd performances, he was not. He fully mastered neither novel, poem, nor academic discourse. Instead, he poured forth a wealth of suggestion, stimulation, and challenge, sometimes with surpassing rhetorical power. But who is to say that our forms are final, and that he did not create in his individualistic fiction, his brilliant controversial and intellectual maneuvering, a kind of unique art which is justified by the response it creates in us? Certainly we should not worship this oddly dedicated man who fought for his own characteristic salvation. If we did, we would earn his scorn. We can learn from him, however, what a human being can achieve. He will assuredly continue to live "on lips of living men."

Notes and References

Chapter One

1. Two excellent bibliographies list the critical studies of Butler as well as his works: A. J. Hoppé, *A Bibliography of the Writings of Samuel Butler (Author of Erewhon) and of Writings about Him* (London, 1925); S. B. Harkness, *The Career of Samuel Butler, 1835-1902, a Bibliography* (London, 1935). Critical discussions since about 1953 are listed in various numbers of *English Fiction in Transition* (Purdue Univ., Lafayette, Indiana), especially Vol. I, No. 1 (Fall-Winter, 1957).

2. Opposing explanations of Butler are found in such studies as Henry Festing Jones, *Samuel Butler, Author of Erewhon (1835-1902) —a Memoir* (London, 1919); Mrs. R. S. Garnett, *Samuel Butler and His Family Relations* (London and Toronto, 1926); Malcolm Muggeridge, *A Study of Samuel Butler, the Earnest Atheist* (London, 1936); and P. N. Furbank, *Samuel Butler, 1835-1902* (Cambridge, England, 1948).

3. The three books which he did not finance are *A First Year in Canterbury Settlement* (published by his father); *Erewhon Revisited* (George Bernard Shaw persuaded Grant Richards to publish it); and *The Way of All Flesh* (published after his death).

4. Philip Henderson called his study *Samuel Butler, The Incarnate Bachelor* (London, 1953), the phrase having originated with the ladies at Heatherley's Art School (H. F. Jones, I, 140).

5. H. F. Jones, I, 212-13.

6. Page references keyed into the text are to *The Shrewsbury Edition of the Works of Samuel Butler,* edited by Henry Festing Jones and A. T. Bartholomew (London, 1923-1926).

7. For example, Sister Mary Bernetta Quinn, O.S.F., "Ernest Pontifex as Antihero," *English Fiction in Transition,* V, 1 (1962), 30-31.

8. *Samuel Butler, 1835-1902,* p. 22.

9. Editha and Richard Sterba, *Beethoven and His Nephew* (New York, 1954).

10. Fyodor Dostoevsky, *Crime and Punishment* (New York, 1928), pp. 107-08.

11. Butler's family background is given in H. F. Jones, I, 1-17.

12. H. F. Jones, II, 265.

13. In a note written in October, 1883, Butler says: "I could publish my novel which is all ready for the press, and so keep myself before the public, but as long as my father lives how can I do this?" MS *Note-Books*, Vol. II, p. 8.

14. *Samuel Butler and His Family Relations.*

15. Jerome Hamilton Buckley, *The Victorian Temper* (Cambridge, Mass., 1951), pp. 117-18.

16. H. F. Jones, I, 39.

17. *Ibid.,* p. 60.

18. For another example of this see *Alps and Sanctuaries,* p. 7.

19. H. F. Jones, I, 58.

20. "A Clergyman's Doubts," the *Examiner* (February 15, 1879).

21. H. F. Jones, I, 59.

22. This idea is used in *The Fair Haven* and is hinted at in *Erewhon,* p. 29.

23. H. F. Jones, I, 61.

24. *The Family Letters of Samuel Butler,* Arnold Silver, ed. (Stanford, Calif., 1962), pp. 74-75.

25. *Ibid.,* p. 76.

26. *Ibid.,* p. 76.

27. *Ibid.,* p. 79.

28. H. F. Jones, I, 89-95.

29. *Ibid.,* p. 71.

30. *Ibid.,* pp. 97, 74.

31. Silver, p. 158.

32. *Samuel Butler and "The Way of All Flesh"* (London, 1947), pp. 44-45.

33. Vol. II, 101, 149; III, 18.

34. H. F. Jones, I, 72, 73; also I, xi.

35. See also Silver, p. 106.

36. (Austin, Texas, 1959).

37. (London, 1912). Quoted in H. F. Jones, I, 87.

38. (London, 1874). Quoted in Joseph Jones, *The Cradle of Erewhon* (Austin, Texas, 1959), p. 52.

39. H. F. Jones, I, 96. See also Silver, pp. 104-05.

40. H. F. Jones, I, 97.

41. *Ibid.,* p. 98.

42. *Ibid.,* p. 99.

43. H. F. Jones, I, 100.

44. *The Press* (April 28, 1863). Quoted by Joseph Jones.

45. H. F. Jones, II, 284-87.

46. *Ibid.,* I, 115.

47. *Ibid.*, pp. 59, 117.
48. *Ibid.*, p. 117.
49. *Ibid.*, p. 118.
50. *Ibid.*, p. 118.
51. *Ibid.*, p. 122.
52. *Ibid.*, p. 123.

Chapter Two

1. H. F. Jones, I, 132-33.
2. *Ibid.*, p. 357.
3. *Samuel Butler and E. M. A. Savage, Letters, 1871-1885*, Geoffrey Keynes and Brian Hill, eds. (London, 1935).
4. H. F. Jones, I, 144.
5. *Ibid.*, pp. 224, 444-48.
6. *Ibid.*, pp. 148-49.
7. *Ibid.*, pp. 154-55.
8. See Lee Elbert Holt, "Samuel Butler's Revisions of *Erewhon*," *Papers of the Bibliographical Society of America*, XXXVIII (1944), 22-38.
9. H. F. Jones, I, 152.
10. H. F. Jones, II, 330-31.
11. April 20, 1872, p. 492.
12. LVI (July, 1872), 137.
13. XVII (May, 1872), 609-10.
14. (April 20, 1872), 507-08.
15. "The New Gulliver," XLV (April 20, 1872), 492-94.
16. H. F. Jones, I, 156.

Chapter Three

1. H. F. Jones, I, 159-60.
2. See, for example, a letter to Mr. Fleay, March 24, 1873, in which Butler explains that he hopes to make a row (Butler Collection, Chapin Library).
3. Philip Henry Gosse, *Omphalos* (London, 1857). For an excellent summary of the conflict between religion and science of the period see Edmund Gosse, *Father and Son* (New York, 1907), especially Chapter V.
4. Professor William Ellery Leonard once told me that he had heard James praise Butler, but I know of no written evidence that James had read him. In July of 1884, however, Butler wrote a long note approving of James' contention (in an article in *Mind*, April, 1884) that we do not cry because we are sad, but are sad because we cry (MS *Note-Books*, Vol. II, p. 77, Chapin Library).
5. H. F. Jones, I, 182.

6. *Ibid.*, p. 175.
7. (February 7, 1874).
8. H. F. Jones, I, 186-87.

Chapter Four

1. H. F. Jones, II, 311.
2. *Ibid.*, I, 202.
3. *Ibid.*, pp. 206-07.
4. Silver, pp. 158-59.
5. H. F. Jones, I, 216.
6. *Ibid.*, p. 214.
7. Silver, p. 161.
8. H. F. Jones, I, 390.
9. *Ibid.*, II, 1. See also two sonnets, "Remorse," *Note-Books*, p. 424.
10. *Ibid.*, I, 233.
11. *Ibid.*, pp. 242-43.
12. *Ibid.*, p. 288.
13. Gertrude Himmelfarb, *Darwin and the Darwinian Revolution* (New York, 1959), p. 419, quoting J. Gray in *Nature*, CLXXIII (1954), 227.
14. *Darwin and Butler—Two Versions of Evolution* (London, 1960), p. 83.
15. *Ibid.*, p. 47.
16. See *Further Extracts from the Note-Books of Samuel Butler* (London, 1934), p. 54.
17. H. F. Jones, I, 264.
18. *Origin of Species* (London, 1876), p. 233. Quoted by Butler, *Life and Habit*, p. 197.
19. Review in *The Athenaeum* (January 26, 1878), pp. 118-19.
20. Review in the *Contemporary Review*, XXXII (May, 1878), 406.
21. Review in the *Westminister Review*, CIX (April, 1878), 240-41.
22. Review in the *Saturday Review*, XVL (January 26, 1878), 119-21.
23. Review in the *Spectator* (February 9, 1878).
24. Review in *Nature*, XIX (March 27, 1879), 477-80.

Chapter Five

1. Basil Willey, among others, accepts Butler's analysis of Buffon, *Darwin and Butler—Two Versions of Evolution*, p. 76.
2. Jonathan Swift, *Gulliver's Travels*, Chapter Five, "A Voyage to Laputa."
3. *The Academy*, XV (May 17, 1879), 426-27.
4. *Nature*, XX (June 12, 1879), 141-44.

5. See H. F. Jones, II, appendix C, 446-67, for a complete account of this affair.

6. *Ibid.*, I, 323.

7. *The Athenaeum* (January 31, 1880).

8. For additional information on the misunderstanding unknown to Jones see *The Autobiography of Charles Darwin, 1809-1882,* Nora Barlow, ed. (London, 1959).

9. *Ibid.*, p. 186.

10. *Ibid.*, p. 216.

11. H. F. Jones, I, 332.

12. The impression has stuck; Gertrude Himmelfarb calls him this in *Darwin and the Darwinian Revolution* (New York, 1959), p. 414.

13. This is Malcolm Muggeridge's thesis in *The Earnest Atheist.*

14. Karl Robert Edouard von Hartmann, *Philosophy of the Unconscious,* (London, 1869). It is interesting to note that C. G. Jung in his *Psychology of the Unconscious* (New York, 1931) finds "a deep psychologic justification" for part of the von Hartmann view (p. 198); but in *Psychological Types* (New York, 1933) he says he is not "a frank adherent of the Hartmann philosophy" (p. 209). Later, however, he links it with his "collective unconscious" in *The Integration of the Personality* (New York, 1939), p. 52.

15. *The Athenaeum* (December 18, 1880), p. 810.

16. *Nature,* XXII (January 27, 1881), 285-87.

17. H. F. Jones, I, 349-50.

18. *The Athenaeum* (March 1, 1884,) pp. 282-83.

19. *The Athenaeum* (March 8, 1884), pp. 312-13.

Chapter Six

1. H. F. Jones, I, 404.

2. *The Athenaeum* (March 22, 1884), pp. 378-79.

3. In a letter in *Nature* (August 12, 1866).

4. Published in 1909.

5. *The Athenaeum* (January 22, 1887), pp. 131-32.

6. *The Athenaeum* (April 13, 1887). Quoted in H. F. Jones, II, 49.

7. *The Academy,* XXX (December 18, 1886), 413.

Chapter Seven

1. H. F. Jones, I, 236, 384.

2. *Ibid.*, pp. 384-85.

3. September 18, 1890. MS in the Chapin Library Collection.

4. H. F. Jones, I, 251.

5. *Ibid.*, p. 334.

6. *Ibid.*, p. 356.

Chapter Eight

1. H. F. Jones, I, 202.
2. *Ibid.*, p. 303.
3. *Ibid.*, p. 391.
4. *Ibid.*, p. 398.
5. *Ibid.*, p. 398.
6. *Ibid.*, p. 216.
7. *Ibid.*, pp. 389-90.
8. John Henry Raleigh, "Victorian Morals and the Modern Novel," *Partisan Review*, XXV (Spring, 1958), 241-64.
9. U. C. Knoepflmacher, "Ishmael or Anti-hero? The Division of Self in *The Way of All Flesh*," *English Fiction in Transition*, VI, No. iii (1961), 29.
10. MS letter in Chapin Library Collection.
11. The original letter is given in Silver, pp. 40-42.
12. *Ibid.*, p. 12.
13. Furbank makes a special point of this.
14. The thesis that Butler did not recognize the importance of art as Joyce did is developed in Ilse Dusoir Lind, "*The Way of All Flesh* and *A Portrait of the Artist as a Young Man:* a Comparison," *The Victorian Newsletter*, IX (Spring, 1956), 7-10.

Chapter Nine

1. Carroll Wilson speculates, in a note in the Chapin Library Collection, that just before his death Butler made Streatfeild rather than Jones his literary executor because he knew that the former would be able to publish *The Way of All Flesh* immediately, whereas Jones, who was acquainted with Butler's sisters, would not.
2. Basil Willey calls these the "three great explosions . . . which rocked the fabric of Christendom and sent believers scuttling for shelter." *Darwin and Butler—Two Versions of Evolution* (London, 1960), p. 9.
3. A letter Butler wrote to Mr. Fleay, March 24, 1873, in the Chapin Library Collection, shows that he clearly wanted to make trouble.
4. H. F. Jones, II, 49.
5. Henry Festing Jones, "Sketch of the Life of Samuel Butler," *Selected Essays by Samuel Butler* (London, 1927), p. 43.
6. Basil Willey comments on the open agreement between Darwin and Wallace to share credit for the survival-of-the-fittest theory: "All honour to such men, and to the Victorian age that produced them. The Cause of science . . . derived great strength . . . from the moral nobility of its champions." p. 12. How Butler would have winced at this!

7. H. F. Jones, II, 54.

8. In a note on April 18, 1893, Butler says that he chose "the fighting road rather than the hang-on-to-a-great-man road" and suffered accordingly. *The Notebooks*, 381.

9. H. F. Jones, I, 145.

10. Furbank believes that this is characteristic of Butler, *Samuel Butler, 1835-1902*, p. 21.

11. The *Spectator*, LXI (August 4, 1888), 1065.

12. Passages like this give credence to Furbank's suggestion that Butler wanted to destroy science. He certainly did want to destroy pretense in science.

13. H. F. Jones, II, 73.

14. *Ibid.*, I, 237.

15. *Ibid.*, II, 81, 252.

16. *Ibid.*, pp. 198, 227.

17. The *Spectator*, LXXVII (November 21, 1896), 731.

18. *The Athenaeum* (October 24, 1896), 555-56.

19. *The Academy*, L (November 28, 1896), 449.

20. H. F. Jones, II, 259.

Chapter Ten

1. H. F. Jones, II, 105.

2. *Ibid.*, p. 121.

3. *The Athenaeum* (January 30 and February 20, 1892). See H. F. Jones, II, 123-24.

4. *Homer's Daughter* (New York, 1955), p. 9.

5. H. F. Jones, II, 172.

6. *Ibid.*, pp. 207-08.

7. Silver, *The Family Letters of Samuel Butler*, p. 19.

8. Richard Lattimore, for example, says: "And did he [Homer] write both Iliad and Odyssey? This is not a soluble problem and it is not, to me, a very interesting one; it is the work, not the man or men who composed the work, which is interesting." *The Iliad of Homer* (Chicago, 1951), p. 29.

9. The *Saturday Review*, LXXXIV (December 4, 1897), 625-27.

10. *Notes and Queries*, XII, 8th Series (December 4, 1897), 458-59.

11. H. F. Jones, II, 207.

12. *Ibid.*, p. 105.

13. *The Academy*, LV (November 26, 1898), 328-29.

14. *The Athenaeum* (November 12, 1898), 668.

15. *Notes and Queries*, II, 9th Series (November 19, 1898), 419.

16. H. F. Jones, II, 311.

17. The *Spectator*, LXVIII (April 23, 1892), 555-56.

18. H. F. Jones, I, 61.
19. *Ibid.*, II, 128-30.
20. *Ibid.*, p. 351.
21. *Ibid.*, pp. 284-87.
22. *Shakespeare—A Critical Study of His Mind and Art* (London, 1889), pp. 394-402.
23. Rolf-Dietrich Keil says that "In jahrzehntelanger Mosaikarbeit hat Sir Denys Bray schliesslich die Bestätigung seiner Hopothese gefunden," that metrical and verbal links can be used to reestablish the order of the sonnets. I do not believe, however, that Shakespeare scholars have agreed about this. *Shakespeare, die Sonnette* (Düssel-dorf-Köln, 1959), p. 7.
24. *The Academy*, LVIII (January 6, 1900), 13.
25. *Notes and Queries* (November 18, 1899).

Chapter Eleven

1. H. F. Jones, II, 251, 331.
2. *Ibid.*, p. 339.
3. *Samuel Butler's Notebooks*, Geoffrey Keynes and Brian Hill, eds. (New York, [1951]), p. 46.
4. H. F. Jones, II, 339-41.
5. Furbank takes special note of this.
6. One thinks of the Basel drawing, on which an important inscription was "restored" into invisibility. *Collected Essays*, Vol. II, 193ff.
7. *Further Extracts from the Note-Books of Samuel Butler*, p. 26.
8. *Ibid.*, p. 17.
9. The "A" or first copy is in the Chapin Library, Williamstown, Mass.
10. Other extracts are to be found in *Butleriana*, A. T. Bartholomew, ed. (London, 1932); *Further Extracts from the Notebooks of Samuel Butler*, A. T. Bartholomew, ed. (London, 1934); *Samuel Butler's Notebooks*, Geoffrey Keynes and Brian Hill, eds. (New York, [1951]).

Chapter Twelve

1. *The Monthly Review* (September, 1902).
2. *The Athenaeum* (May 30, 1903), No. 3944, p. 683.
3. *The Journals of Arnold Bennett* (London, 1933), Vol. I, 193-94.
4. *The Independent Review* (September, 1914), Vol. III, 527-38.
5. The London *Times Literary Supplement* (October 8, 1908), No. 352.
6. "Heredity and Variation in Modern Lights," *Darwin and Modern Science* (Cambridge, 1909), p. 88.
7. *An Introduction to Biology and Other Papers* (New York, 1917).

8. *Mind* (July, 1914), NS 23, 371-85.

9. *Dublin Review* (October, 1914), Vol. 155, 322-44.

10. *Samuel Butler der Jüngere. Versuch einer Darstellung seiner Gedankenwelt* (Zürich, 1914).

11. *A Defence of Idealism* (London, 1917).

12. *Modern English Writers* (London, 1918), p. 327.

13. *Ibid.*, p. 330.

14. "Mr. Gilbert Cannan on Samuel Butler," *The New Statesman* (May 8, 1915), Vol. V, 109-10.

15. *Samuel Butler* (London, 1916).

16. *The Cambridge History of English Literature* (Cambridge, 1916), Vol. XIII, Chap. 14, 499-505.

17. *Ibid.*, p. 505.

18. *The North American Review* (August, 1916), Vol. CCIV, 270-81.

19. "Samuel Butler, the Master Satirist," *As I Was Saying* (Boston, 1923), pp. 52-85.

20. *From Shakespeare to O. Henry* (New York, 1917), pp. 180-220.

21. *Samuel Butler, Author of Erewhon (1835-1902)—a Memoir* (London, 1919).

22. Letter in Chapin Library Butler Collection, from Mrs. Gogin to Robert F. Rattray, May, 1935.

23. The *Manchester Guardian* (November 7, 1919).

24. *The Unpartizan Review* (January 1921), Vol. XV, 20-42; reprinted in *Shelburne Essays, 11th Series* (Boston, 1921), pp. 167-199.

25. (London and Boston, 1924).

26. *Histoire de la Littérature Anglaise* (Paris, 1924) and *Le Roman et les Idées en Angleterre* (Strasbourg, 1923).

27. (London, 1925).

28. (New York, 1932).

29. (London, 1935).

30. *University of Toronto Quarterly* (October 1935), Vol. V, 21-36.

31. (London, 1936).

32. *Samuel Butler, 1835-1902* (Cambridge, England, 1948).

33. (London, 1939).

34. *Samuel Butler, 1835-1902.*

35. *Samuel Butler, the Incarnate Bachelor* (London, 1953).

36. For example, Walter Allen, *The English Novel, a Short Critical History* (London, 1954); Ellen Douglass Leyburn, *Satiric Allegory: Mirror of Man,* Yale Studies in English, CXXX, 1956; William H. Marshall, "*The Way of All Flesh:* The Dual Function of Edward Overton," The University of Texas *Studies in Literature and Language,* Vol. IV, No. 4, 1963.

37. See, for example, Clara Stillman, *Samuel Butler, a Mid-Victorian Modern* (New York, 1932).

38. For an analysis of the basic tenets of Victorianism, see Walter E. Houghton, *The Victorian Frame of Mind—1830-1870* (New Haven, 1957).

39. See G. M. Young, *Victorian England, Portrait of an Age* (London, 1953), and Elie Halévy, *A History of the English People in the Nineteenth Century—IV, Victorian Years* (New York, 1961).

40. In an unpublished note written in 1884 (MS *Notebooks*, Vol. I, p. 97, Chapin Library, Williamstown, Mass.) Butler wonders why he has been greeted by "more hisses than applause," but consoles himself with the reflection that in the London of his time he has "everything that makes life worth living."

Selected Bibliography

PRIMARY SOURCES

Books, articles, and published letters by Samuel Butler

The following items were written sometime between 1854 and 1859. Place of first publication is given for each one.
"The Battle of Alma Mater," *Shrewsbury Edition*, I, 50.
"An Eminent Person," *Shrewsbury Edition*, I, 44.
"On the Italian Priesthood," *The Note-Books of Samuel Butler* (London, 1912), p. 388.
"Napoleon at St. Helena," *The Eagle* (December, 1902).
"Powers," *Shrewsbury Edition*, I, 35.
"Prospectus of the Great Split Society," *The Eagle* (June, 1913).
"The Shield of Achilles, with Variations," *The Eagle* (December, 1902).
"A Skit on Examinations," *The Eagle* (June, 1913).
"Translation from an Unpublished Work of Herodotus," *The Note-Books of Samuel Butler* (London, 1912), p. 384.
"The Two Deans," *The Eagle* (March, 1903).
"The Two Deans, II," *The Note-Books of Samuel Butler* (London, 1912), p. 387.
"Parody of a Simeonite Broadside," written March 31, 1855; first published *The Cambridge Magazine* (March, 1913).
"On English Composition and Other Matters," signed "Cellarius," *The Eagle*, I, No. 1 (Lent term, 1858), 41-44.
"Our Tour," *The Eagle*, I, No. 5 (Easter term, 1859), 241-55.
"Our Emigrant," signed "Cellarius," *The Eagle*, II, 101, 149 and III, 18.
"Darwin on the Origin of Species: a Dialogue," *The Press* (New Zealand) (December 20, 1862).
"Darwin on Species," letters to *The Press*, signed "A. M." (February 21, 1863), (March 18, 1863), (June 22, 1863).
"Darwin among the Machines," signed "Cellarius," *The Press* (June 13, 1863).
A First Year in Canterbury Settlement, privately printed by Longman, Green, Longman, Roberts and Green, 1863.

"The English Cricketers," *The Press* (February 15, 1864).

"A Note on *The Tempest,* Act III, Sc. i," *Literary Foundlings: Verse and Prose Collected in Canterbury, N. Z.* (March, 1864).

"The Mechanical Creation," *The Reasoner* (July 1, 1865).

"Lucubratio Ebria," *The Press* (July 29, 1865).

"Precaution in Free Thought," *The Reasoner* (August 1, 1965).

"The Evidence for the Resurrection of Jesus Christ as Given by the Four Evangelists, Critically Examined," privately printed pamphlet, 1865.

"Dedomenici da Rosa," *The Drawing-Room Gazette* (September 30, 1871).

"Instead of an Article on the Dudley Exhibition," *The Drawing-Room Gazette* (November 11, 1871).

"The Performance of *Jephtha* at Exeter Hall," *The Drawing-Room Gazette* (November 25, 1871).

"The Performance of *Israel in Egypt* at Exeter Hall," *The Drawing-Room Gazette* (December 2, 1871).

"Handel's *Deborah* and Bach's *Passion,*" *The Drawing-Room Gazette* (March 2, 1872).

Erewhon, or Over the Range. London: Trübner, 1872.

The Fair Haven. London: Trübner, 1873.

Letter to the Editor of the *Spectator,* 2369:1470-71 (November 22, 1873).

"Free Thinking and Plain Speaking," the *Examiner* (December 20, 1873).

"Canada Tanning Extract Company Pamphlet," 1875.

Life and Habit. London: Trübner, 1878 (issued December 4, 1877).

Letter concerning Hering and Erasmus Darwin, *The Athenaeum,* 2624:189 (February 9, 1878).

"A Psalm of Montreal," the *Spectator* (May 18, 1878).

Evolution, Old and New. London: Hardwicke and Bogue, 1879. American edition, Salem, Mass.: S. E. Cassino, 1879. Only Butler book published in America before 1910.

"A Clergyman's Doubts," letters in the *Examiner* (February 15, 22; March 1, 8, 15, 22, 29; April 5, 19; May 10, 17; June 14, 18, 1879).

Letter answering Alfred R. Wallace's review of *Evolution, Old and New* in *Nature* for June 12, 1879, *Nature,* XX, 169 (June 19, 1879).

"God the Known and God the Unknown," the *Examiner* (May 24, 31; June 14, 21, 28; July 12, 19, 26, 1879).

Unconscious Memory. London: David Bogue, 1880.

"Evolution Old and New," *The Athenaeum,* 2726:155 (January 31, 1880)

"Mr. Darwin and Mr. Butler," *St. James Gazette* (December 2, 1880).

"Prospectus for *Alps and Sanctuaries*," 1882.

Alps and Sanctuaries. London: David Bogue, 1882 (issued 1881).

"Mr. S. Butler's Unconscious Memory," *Nature*, XXIII (February 3, 1881), 312-13.

Selections from Previous Works. London: Trübner, 1884.

"Mr. Samuel Butler Writes," *The Athenaeum* (January 26, 1884) 2935:124.

"Mental Evolution in Animals," *The Athenaeum* (March 15, 1884) 2942:348-49.

Gavottes, Minuets, Fugues, etc. London: Novello, Ewer and Co., 1885 (with Henry Festing Jones).

"Holbein's 'La Danse,'" pamphlet. London: Trübner, 1886.

"Portraits of Gentile and Giovanni Bellini," *The Athenaeum* (February 20, 1886) 3043:271.

"Holbein's Dance," *The Athenaeum* (October 23, 1886) 3078:282-83.

"To the Electors of the Slade Professor of Fine Art," pamphlet. 1886.

"The Sub-Division of the Organic World into Animal and Vegetable," *Science and Art* (April, June, 1887).

Narcissus. Words of the Choruses, 1887. Pianoforte Score, 1888. Complete edition, 1888 (with Henry Festing Jones).

"Erasmus Darwin and *Evolution, Old and New*," *The Academy* (December 17, 1887).

Luck, or Cunning? London: Trübner, 1887 (issued 1886).

"Mr. Darwin and Mr. Samuel Butler," *The Athenaeum* (November 26, 1887) 3135:716.

Letter, *The Academy* (December 17, 1887) 815:410-11.

Ex Voto. London: Trübner, 1888.

"Quis Desiderio?," *Universal Review* (July, 1888).

"A Sculptor and a Shrine," *Universal Review* (November, 1888).

"The Aunt, the Nieces, and the Dog," *Universal Review* (May, 1889).

"L'Affaire Holbein-Rippel," *Universal Review* (November, 1889).

"A Medieval Girl School," *Universal Review* (December, 1889).

"The Deadlock in Darwinism," *Universal Review* (April, May, June, 1890).

"Art in the Valley of the Saas," *Universal Review* (November, 1890).

"Ramblings in Cheapside," *Universal Review* (December, 1890).

"The Humour of Homer," *The Eagle* (March, 1892) 17:158-193.

A Lecture on the Humour of Homer. Cambridge: Metcalfe, 1892.

Letters on Homer, *The Athenaeum* (January 30, February 20, 1892).

Letters and articles in Italian on the authoress of the *Odyssey, Il Lambruschini*, Trapani, June, 1892-September, 1894.

Letter on the Sacro Monte of Varallo, the *Times* (October 17, 1892).

"On the Trapanese Origin of the *Odyssey*," *The Eagle*, XVII (December, 1892), 353-365.

On the Trapanese Origin of the Odyssey. Cambridge: Metcalfe and Co., 1893.

Sample Passages from a New Prose Translation of the Odyssey. Edinburgh: T. and A. Constable, 1893.

"L'Origine Siciliana dell' Odissea," *Rassegne della Litteratura Siciliana*, Acireale, 1893.

"A Translation Attempted in Consequence of a Challenge," *The Eagle*, XVIII (March, 1894), 131.

"Ancora sull' Origine Siciliana dell' Odissea," *Rassegna della Litteratura Siciliana*, Acireale, 1894.

"On the Sicilian Origin of the Odyssey," *Italian Gazette*, Rome (February 9, 23; March 16, 23, 30, 1895).

"A New Prose Translation of Homer," Extracts with comments, *The Eagle*, XVIII (March, 1895), 484-88.

Letters in debate with William Ridgeway on "Writing in Homer," *The Academy* (July 20; August 3, 17, 31, 1895).

"The Birds of Antiquity," *The Athenaeum* (March 21, 1896), 3569: 385-86.

The Life and Letters of Dr. Samuel Butler. London: John Murray, 1896.

The Authoress of the Odyssey. London: Longmans, 1897.

"Shakespeare's Sonnets," *The Athenaeum* (July 30, 1897), 3692:161.

The Iliad of Homer. London: Longmans, 1898.

"Shakespeare's Sonnets and the Ireland Forgeries," *The Athenaeum* (December 24, 1898), 3713:907-08.

"The Only Begetter," *The Athenaeum* (January 21, 1899), 3717:92.

Shakespeare's Sonnets Reconsidered. London: Longmans, 1899.

"'Beget' and 'Begetter' in Elizabethan English," *The Athenaeum* (March 10, 1900), 3776:315-16; (March 24, 1900), 3778:379-80.

The Odyssey Rendered into English Prose. London: Longmans, 1900.

"The σέλινον of the Greeks," *The Atheneaum* (July 13, 1901), 3847: 61.

Erewhon Revisited. London: Grant Richards, 1901.

"La Nuova Quistione Omerica: Le Autore dell' Odissea E una Donna?," *Quo Vadis?* (October 4, 1901).

"Erewhon Revisited," *Daily News* (November 1, 1901), 8.

"Bacon-Shakespeare," the *Times* (December 31, 1901), 10.

"Not on Sad Stygian Shore," *The Athenaeum* (January 6, 1902), 3871:18.

"Erewhon and The Spectator," the *Spectator* (February 15, 1902), 3842:253.

Selected Bibliography

Letter, *Quo Vadis?* (July 12, 1902).

The Way of All Flesh. London: Grant Richards, 1903.

Seven Sonnets and a Psalm of Montreal. Cambridge, 1904.

Essays on Life, Art, and Science. London: Grant Richards, 1904.

Ulysses. London: Weeks, 1904 (with Henry Festing Jones).

"The Note-Books," *New Quarterly Review,* Nos. 1-4, 6, 9, 10 (1907-1910).

The Note-Books of Samuel Butler. London: Fifield, 1912.

The Shrewsbury Edition. Henry Festing Jones and A. T. Bartholomew, eds. London and New York: Jonathan Cape and E. P. Dutton, 1923-1926.

Butleriana. A. T. Bartholomew, ed., London: Nonesuch Press, 1932.

Further Extracts from the Note-Books of Samuel Butler. A. T. Bartholomew, ed., London: Jonathan Cape, 1934.

Samuel Butler and E. M. A. Savage, Letters 1871-1885. Geoffrey Keynes and Brian Hill, eds. London: Jonathan Cape, 1935.

Samuel Butler's Note Books. Geoffrey Keynes and Brian Hill, eds. London: Jonathan Cape, 1951.

The Family Letters of Samuel Butler. Arnold Silver, ed. Stanford, Calif., 1962.

The Correspondence of Samuel Butler and His Sister May. Daniel F. Howard, ed. Berkeley, Calif.: Univ. of California Press, 1962.

SECONDARY SOURCES

These selected books and articles on Butler, or dealing with him in part, are a starting point for the student who wishes to become better acquainted with Butler criticism.

Allen, Walter. *The English Novel, a Short Critical History.* London: Phoenix, 1954. A good example of a recent appraisal of Butler's influence on the English novel.

Bateson, W. *Darwin and Modern Science.* Cambridge, England: Cambridge University Press, 1910. First scientific discussion to pay close attention to Butler's *Life and Habit* theory.

Bekker, W. G. *An Historical and Critical Review of Samuel Butler's Literary Works.* Rotterdam: Nijgh and Van Ditmar, 1925. A serious attempt to find unity and value in Butler's works.

Bennett, Arnold. *The Journals of Arnold Bennett.* New York: Viking Press, 1932. Comments on Butler here and there show the effect he had on Bennett.

Bissell, Clyde T. "A Study of *The Way of All Flesh,*" *Nineteenth Century Studies,* Herbert Davis, ed. Ithaca: Cornell University Press, 1940. Butler's novel interpreted in the light of his theory of evolution.

Blum, Jean. "Samuel Butler," *Mercure de France* (July-August, 1910). An early article introducing French readers to Butler and praising him for his broad humanism.

Böttgar, Heinz. *Samuel Butlers satirische Romane und ihre literarische Bedeutung.* Marburg: R. Berger in Luca, 1936. An analysis of Butler as satirist.

Butler, Samuel. *The Essential Samuel Butler.* Selected and with an introduction by G. D. H. Cole, New York: E. P. Dutton, [1950]. The introduction treats Butler lightly but well.

————. *The Shrewsbury Edition.* Henry Festing Jones and A. T. Bartholomew, eds. London and New York: Jonathan Cape and E. P. Dutton, 1923-1926. Introductions to the volumes provide much important bibliographical and background material.

Cannan, Gilbert. *Samuel Butler, a Critical Study.* London: M. Secker, 1915. This first booklength study of Butler fails to see him as a whole, but contains many telling insights.

Cazamian, Madeleine L. *Le Roman et les Idées en Angleterre. L'Influence de la Science, 1860-1890.* Strasbourg: Librarie Istra, 1923. Chapter III, pp. 172-238, attempts to see Butler as a product of the times in which he lived.

Clutton-Brock, A. *Essays on Books.* London: Methuen and Co., 1921. Reprints Clutton-Brock's early articles on Butler from the *Times.*

Cole, G. D. H. *Samuel Butler and "The Way of All Flesh."* London: Home and Van Thal, 1947. A lively but casual discussion of Butler.

Darbishire, A. D. *An Introduction to Biology and Other Papers.* London: Cassell, 1917. Excellent example of the really profound influence exerted by Butler's work on one biologist.

Darwin, Charles. *The Autobiography of Charles Darwin.* Nora Barlow, ed. New York: Harcourt, 1959. This recent edition throws new light on Butler's quarrel with Darwin.

Drummond, Andrew L. *The Churches in English Fiction.* Leicester: E. Bakus, 1950. Interesting use of *The Way of All Flesh* for sociological background.

Farrington, B. *Samuel Butler and the Odyssey.* London: Jonathan Cape, 1929. Argues for acceptance of Butler's Homeric theories.

Flaccus, Louis W. "Samuel Butler," *University of Pennsylvania Lectures, 1918-1919, VI.* Philadelphia: University of Pennsylvania Press. A good general appraisal.

Fort, Joseph. *Samuel Butler, L'écrivain; Étude d'un Style.* Bordeaux: J. Bière, 1935. Concludes that, although Butler used words cleverly and with a real sense of their meaning, he lacked a genuine style.

————. *Samuel Butler (1835-1902), Étude d'un Caractère et d'un*

Intelligence. Bordeaux: J. Bière, 1935. Considers Butler valuable for his ideas and his personality, not for his creative ability.

Frierson, William C. *The English Novel in Transition.* Norman, Oklahoma: University of Oklahoma Press, 1942. Suggests that Butler contributed to the reaction against objectivity in the English novel.

Frye, Northrop. *Anatomy of Criticism.* Princeton: Princeton University Press, 1957. Interesting references to Butler as a satirist.

————. "The Four Forms of Prose Fiction," *Hudson Review,* II (1950), 582-95.

Furbank, P. N. *Samuel Butler, 1835-1902.* Cambridge, England: Cambridge University Press, 1948. Thoughtful, recent study which makes many telling points, but rejects most of Butler.

Garnett, R. S. *Samuel Butler and His Family Relations.* London and Toronto: J. M. Dent, 1926. An attempt to demonstrate that Butler misrepresented his family in *The Way of All Flesh.*

Gerould, Gordon Hall. *The Patterns of English and American Fiction.* Boston: Little, Brown, 1942. Praises the structure of *The Way of All Flesh.*

Harkness, Stanley B. *The Career of Samuel Butler, 1835-1902: a Bibliography.* New York: Macmillan, 1956. Definitive bibliography.

Harris, John F. *Samuel Butler, Author of Erewhon.* London: G. Richards, 1916. Early appreciative study, not so partisan as Gilbert Cannan's.

Henderson, Philip. *Samuel Butler, the Incarnate Bachelor.* London: Cohen and West, 1953. Generally agreed to be the best recent biography. Little attention paid to Butler's ideas.

Henkin, Leo J. *Darwinism in the English Novel.* New York: Corporate Press, 1940. Discusses *The Way of All Flesh* as a carrying out of Butler's theory of evolution.

Hicks, Granville. *Figures of Transition.* New York: Macmillan, 1939.

Himmelfarb, Gertrude. *Darwin and the Darwinian Revolution.* New York: Doubleday, 1959. Passing comments on Butler's evolution theory.

Holt, Lee Elbert. "Samuel Butler and His Victorian Critics," *Journal of English Literary History,* VIII, No. 2 (June, 1941), 146-59.

————. "Samuel Butler's Rise to Fame," *Publications of the Modern Language Association,* LVII, No. 3 (September, 1942), 867-78.

————. "Samuel Butler's Revisions of *Erewhon*," *Papers of the Bibliographical Society of America,* XXXVIII (1944), 22-38.

————. "The Note-Books of Samuel Butler," *Publications of the Modern Language Association,* LX, No. 4 (December, 1945), 1165-79.

Hoppé, A. J. *A Bibliography of the Writings of Samuel Butler*. London: Bookman's, [1925].

Howard, Daniel, "The Critical Significance of Autobiography in *The Way of All Flesh*," *Victorian Newsletter*, No. 17 (Spring, 1960).

Irvine, William. *The Universe of G. B. S.* New York: Whittlesey House, 1949. Many interesting comments on Butler's influence on Shaw.

Joad, C. E. M. *Samuel Butler, 1835-1902*. London: L. Parsons, 1924. Enthusiastic account of Butler's biological theories.

Jones, Henry Festing. *Charles Darwin and Samuel Butler*. London: A. C. Fifield, 1911. Presents facts of Butler's quarrel with Darwin.

————. *Samuel Butler, Author of Erewhon (1835-1902)—a Memoir*. London: Macmillan, 1919. Storehouse of biographical information, but not notable for objective character portrayal.

————, and A. T. Bartholomew. *The Samuel Butler Collection at Saint John's College, Cambridge*. Cambridge, England: W. Heffer and Sons, 1921.

Jones, Joseph Jay. *The Cradle of Erewhon: Samuel Butler in New Zealand*. Austin, Texas: University of Texas Press, 1959. Some interesting new sidelights on Butler's years in New Zealand.

Kettle, Arnold. *An Introduction to the English Novel*. London: Hutchinson, 1953.

Knoepflmacher, V. C. "Ishmael or Anti-hero? The Division of Self in *The Way of All Flesh*." *English Fiction in Transition*, IV, No. iii (1961), 28-35. Analysis of the points of view from which the novel is written.

Kogan, Bernard R. *Darwin and His Critics: The Darwinian Revolution*. San Francisco: Wadsworth, 1960. Sourcebook which makes use of material from Butler.

Lange, Petronella Jacoba de. *Samuel Butler, Critic and Philosopher*. Zutphen: W. J. Thieme, 1925. Thoughtful appraisal of Butler's point of view, commending him for his openmindedness and his reaction against materialism.

Larbaud, Valery. "Samuel Butler," *La Nouvelle Revue Français*, XIV (January-June, 1920). The French translator of Butler discusses his work.

————. "Samuel Butler," *Revue de France* (October 1, 1923).

LeRoy, Gaylord C. *Perplexed Prophets. Six Nineteenth Century British Authors*. Philadelphia: Temple University Publications, 1953.

Leyburn, Ellen Douglass. *Satiric Allegory: Mirror of Man*. Yale Studies in English, CXXX. New Haven, Conn.: Yale University Press, 1956. Praises *Erewhon* for range of satiric ideas and for its unity of conception.

Selected Bibliography

Lind, Ilse Dusoir. *"The Way of All Flesh* and *A Portrait of the Artist as a Young Man:* A Comparison." *The Victorian Newsletter* (Spring, 1956).

Lunn, Hugh Kingsmill. *After Puritanism (1850-1900).* London: Duckworth, 1929. Attack on Butler based on the conviction that his emotional life was seriously disturbed.

MacCarthy, Desmond. *Remnants.* London: Constable, 1918. Some firsthand memories of Butler.

Mais, S. P. B. *From Shakespeare to O. Henry.* New York: Dodd, Mead, 1917. Butler praised for being a great Puritan.

Marshall, William H. *"The Way of All Flesh:* The Dual Function of Edward Overton," *Studies in Literature and Language,* IV, No. 4 (Winter, 1963).

McCann, Charles, "Portraits of the Artists as Young Men: Fact versus Fiction," *English Fiction in Transition,* V, No. 1 (1962).

Meissner, Paul. *Samuel Butler der Jüngere.* Leipzig: Tauchnitz, 1931. Serious academic study; sets Butler in the context of his time, but rejects much of him.

More, Paul Elmer. *Shelburne Essays, Eleventh Series.* Boston: Houghton, Mifflin, 1921.

Muggeridge, Malcolm. *A Study of Samuel Butler, the Earnest Atheist.* London: G. P. Putnam, 1936. A damaging caricature of Butler, directed more at his hero-worshipers than at him.

O'Connor, William van. "Samuel Butler and Bloomsbury." *From Jane Austin to Joseph Conrad.* Robert C. Rathburn and Martin Steinman, Jr., eds. Minneapolis: University of Minnesota Press, 1958.

O'Neill, H. C. "Samuel Butler." *The Great Victorians.* H. J. and Hugh Massingham, eds. London: I. Nicholson and Watson, 1932.

Pestalozzi, Gerold. *Samuel Butler der Jüngere, Versuch einer Darstellung seiner Gedankenwelt.* Zürich: Universität Zürich, 1914. Discusses the ways in which Butler's creative career carries out ideas expressed in *Erewhon.*

Quinn, Sister Mary Bernetta. "Ernest Pontifex as Anti-hero," *English Fiction in Transition,* V, No. 1 (1962).

Rattray, R. F. *Samuel Butler: A Chronicle and an Introduction.* London: Duckworth, 1935.

Routh, H. V. *Towards the Twentieth Century.* New York: Macmillan, 1937. Links Butler with Nietzsche and Bergson for his attempt to adapt science to humanism, but suggests that he failed because he was not a gifted writer.

Salter, W. H. *Essays on Two Moderns: Euripides, Samuel Butler.* London: Sidgwick and Jackson, 1911. Praises Butler for his universality, but condemns him for his attack on science.

Shafer, Robert. *Christianity and Naturalism*. New Haven: Yale University Press, 1926. Appraises Butler as the detached observer of life.

Shaw, George Bernard. *Back to Methuselah*. New York: Brentano, 1921.

————. *John Bull's Other Island and Major Barbara*. New York: Brentano, 1910.

Sinclair, May. *A Defence of Idealism*. New York: Macmillan, 1917. A direct attack on Butler and all that he stood for.

Somervell, D. C. *English Thought in the Nineteenth Century*. London: Methuen, 1929.

Stillman, Clara G. *Samuel Butler, a Mid-Victorian Modern*. New York: Viking Press, 1932. An analysis of Butler's leading ideas, with emphasis upon their modernity.

Stoff, Rudolf. *Die Philosophie des Organischen bei Samuel Butler*. Vienna: Phaidon Verlag, 1929. A serious attempt to discover a consistent and viable philosophy in Butler's work.

Tax, Sol, ed. *Evolution after Darwin*. Chicago: University of Chicago Press, 1960. A general survey which includes some account of Butler's work.

Wallace, Alfred Russel. *My Life*. New York: Dodd, Mead, 1905.

Willey, Basil. *Darwin and Butler—Two Versions of Evolution*. London: Chatto, 1960. This valuable study strongly suggests that the issues Butler raised are not dead, though Willey rejects Butler's *Life and Habit* theory.

[Wilson, Carroll A.] *Catalogue of the Collection of Samuel Butler (of Erewhon) in the Chapin Library, Williams College*. Portland: The Southworth-Anthoensen Press, 1945.

Wilson, Edmund. *The Triple Thinkers, Ten Essays on Literature*. New York: Harcourt, Brace, 1945.

Zabel, Morton D. *Craft and Character in Modern Fiction*. New York: Viking, 1957. Praises Butler chiefly for the extraordinary power of *The Way of All Flesh*.

Index

Index